make
1-weekend gifts

20+ Thoughtful Projects to Sew

C&T PUBLISHING

Publisher: Amy Barrett-Daffin

Creative Director / Editorial Compiler: Gailen Runge

Senior Acquisitions Editor: Roxane Cerda

Developmental Editors: Liz Aneloski, Cynthia Bix, Joanna Burgarino, S. Michele Fry, Monica Gyulai, Lee Jonsson, Lynn Koolish, and Karla Menaugh

Technical Editors: Carolyn Aune, Mary E. Flynn, Helen Frost, Doreen Hazel, Susan Hendrickson, Linda Johnson, Ellen Pahl, Sandy Peterson, Debbie Rodgers, Daniel Rouse, Gailen Runge, Alison M. Schmidt, Teresa Stroin, Julie Waldman, Janice Wray, and Nanette Zeller

Cover/Book Designer: April Mostek

Production Coordinator: Zinnia Heinzmann

Production Editors: Alice Mace Nakanishi and Jennifer Warren

Illustrators: Freesia Pearson Blizard, Lon Eric Craven, Jenny Davis, Rue Flaherty, Valyrie Gillum, Aneela Hoey, Jessica Jenkins, Linda Johnson, Samarra Khaja, Minki Kim, Tim Manibusan, Wendy Mathson, Eric Sears, Aliza Shalit, Amanda Siegfried, Janice Wray, and Zinnia Heinzmann

Photography Assistant: Gabriel Martinez

Front cover photography by Nissa Brehmer

Interior photography as noted

Published by C&T Publishing, Inc., P.O. Box 1456, Lafayette, CA 94549

Library of Congress Cataloging-in-Publication Data

Names: C & T Publishing, publisher.

Title: Make 1-weekend gifts : 20+ thoughtful projects to sew.

Description: Lafayettee, CA : Stash Books, [2022] | Summary: "Whip up something for everyone on your gift list with this collection of sewing projects! Includes little personal accessories, thoughtful gifts for outdoor adventures, personal touches to brighten a home, and kitchen gifts"-- Provided by publisher.

Identifiers: LCCN 2021053901 | ISBN 9781644032336 (trade paperback) | ISBN 9781644032343 (ebook)

Subjects: LCSH: Sewing. | Gifts.

Classification: LCC TT705 .M27 2022 | DDC 646.2--dc23/eng/20211116

LC record available at https://lccn.loc.gov/2021053901

Printed in the USA

10 9 8 7 6 5 4 3 2 1

Contents

Equinox Greeting Cards

Jen Fox and Sarah Case

FINISHED GREETING CARDS: 5″ × 7″

Greeting cards are a fast, fun project that uses up small scraps of fusible web and fabric. Play with different arrangements of motif pieces to create a set of cards, or try framing a card for inexpensive wall art.

Style photography by Lucy Glover and instructional photography by Diane Pedersen

JEN FOX is Jen Fox is the owner of Jen Fox Studios, an independent sewing pattern and textile design company. Armed with a background in interior design, she began the company while in design school and continues to build it while working full time designing interior spaces for a commercial architecture firm in New Mexico. When she isn't hiking, biking, and exploring the mountains and desert of the southwest, Jen can be found exploring her current city of Albuquerque, New Mexico.

WEBSITE: foxlyhandmade.com

SARAH CASE is an artist, designer, and seamstress. In 2006, she started her own jewelry line. In 2010, fueled by her Textiles and Art degree, her focus turned to a deeper passion for fabric, fibers, design, and experimentation. A love of people, travel, and adventure inspires her work. When she isn't designing, Sarah can be found biking, skiing, knitting, dancing around her kitchen while cooking, or with camera in hand exploring a new place.

This project originally appeared in *Transfer · Embellish · Stitch*, by Jen Fox and Sarah Case, available from Stash Books.

Materials

Transfer method: Fusible web
FUSIBLE WEB: scraps or 1/8 yard

Project
PACKAGE OF BLANK GREETING CARDS:
5″ × 7″

ASSORTED COTTON FABRIC SCRAPS

COORDINATING THREAD

Making the Cards

1. Trace the small Equinox motif (page 88) onto fusible web and roughly cut out.

Follow the manufacturer's instructions to fuse the web to the wrong side of the fabric scraps.

2. Fuse the pieces to the blank greeting cards in any configuration you wish.

3. Add additional design elements by stitching with your sewing machine, using a straight stitch with a long stitch length, either on top of the fused motifs or in the negative space.

tip When sewing paper in a sewing machine, set aside a specific machine needle to be used only with paper, because the tip of the needle will dull more rapidly.

Cards
Amanda Jean Nyberg

Sewing through paper is so much fun. Use tiny fabric scraps to make a card that will bring a smile to someone's face. This is a great way to use scraps that are so small that they can no longer hold a seam allowance. This is just one example of a design. Get creative and come up with your own designs, too.

Style photography by Lucy Glover and instructional photography by Diane Pedersen and Amanda Jean Nyberg

AMANDA JEAN NYBERG grew up in a family of six children, and it comes as no surprise that she is frugal. It is in her blood, whether she likes it or not, and it's reflected in her quiltmaking. Using up every last bit of fabric has become one of the trademarks of her quilts. Given a choice between using scraps or stash, she would choose scraps nine times out of ten.

Amanda Jean, her husband, and their children live in Wisconsin. They love living in a place where the local parade offerings include not only candy but also cheese curds and chocolate milk.

This project originally appeared in *No Scrap Left Behind*, by Amanda Jean Nyberg, available from Stash Books or C&T Publishing.

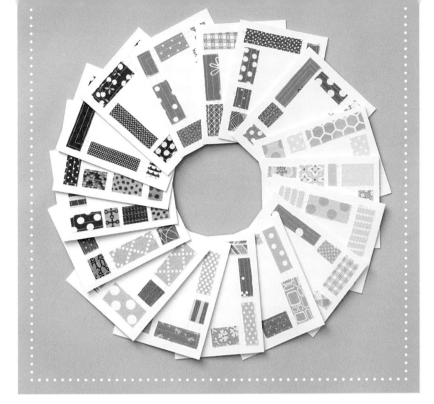

Materials

SMALL SCRAPS IN A VARIETY OF COLORS: Each measuring 1/2"–1 1/2" on each side

8 1/2" × 11" CARD STOCK

THREAD TO MATCH THE CARD STOCK

GLUE STICK

DOUBLE-SIDED TAPE OR A TAPE RUNNER (NORMALLY USED FOR SCRAPBOOKING)

Construction

1. Cut a piece of card stock to 5 1/2" × 8 1/2". Fold it in half so that it measures 5 1/2" × 4 1/4". Set aside.

2. Cut a piece of card stock to 5 1/2" × 4 1/4".

tip Cutting Paper with a Rotary Cutter

Use rotary cutter blades that have become too dull to cut fabric to cut paper instead. This is a great way to cut the card stock pieces quickly and accurately. Consider keeping an extra rotary cutter on hand especially for paper. And be sure to label it.

3. Arrange the scraps of fabric on the 5 1/2" × 4 1/4" piece of card stock. Use a glue stick to hold the fabric pieces in place temporarily.

4. Stitch around the fabric edges to attach the fabric pieces to the card stock permanently. Backstitch (2 or 3 stitches is plenty) at the beginning and end of each seam. Trim the threads as short as possible.

5. Attach the patchwork piece of card stock to the folded card stock with double-sided tape or a tape runner. This will hide the stitching lines and produce a nicely finished card.

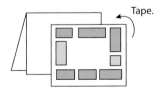

Tape.

6. Write a greeting on the front of the card (such as "hello," "thank you," or "happy birthday"), if desired.

7. Write a message inside and send the card to a friend.

tip Change Your Needle

When you are finished making cards, be sure to change out your sewing needle, which will have become dull after sewing through paper.

Furoshiki Gift-Card Box

Julie Creus

FINISHED BOX:
3½" wide × 2½" tall × 1¼" deep
(fits a standard gift card)

Originating from Japanese culture, which promotes caring for the environment and reducing waste, furoshiki is the eco-friendly wrapping cloth. This project? A fun, reusable fabric-wrapping idea for a gift card or other small gift.

Styled photos by Nissa Brehmer; instructional photos by Diane Pedersen

JULIE CREUS has been dubbed by friends as "La Todera," mistress of all trades. She designs fabrics, teaches craft classes, and creates unique, stylish items with clever construction methods. She lives in Orlando, Florida.

WEBSITE: latodera.com

This project originally appeared in *Adventures in Fabric—La Todera Style*, by Julie M. Creus, available as an eBook from Stash Books.

NOTE: CONSTRUCTION OVERVIEW

Sandwich your favorite cotton quilting fabric with a stiff fusible interfacing. Fold the flaps in upon one another to hide a surprise!

Materials and Cutting

FUROSHIKI GIFT-CARD BOX

Use the Furoshiki Gift-Card Box marking template A and Patterns B, C, D, E, and F (page 89). Trace onto clear template plastic and cut out to create templates A, B, C, D, E, and F.

Fabric	For	Cutting
Fat eighth or ¼ yard fabric	Outer box	Cut 1 rectangle 9″ × 12″.
Fat eighth or ¼ yard fabric	Inner box	Cut 1 rectangle 9″ × 12″.
9″ × 12″ rectangle or a heavy-duty double-sided fusible interfacing (I used Craf-Tex Plus. You also could use fast2fuse HEAVY.)	Interfacing	Cut 1 each from templates B, C, D, E, and F.
Findings: Topstitching thread in colors that coordinate with the outer box fabric		
Tools: Sewing machine, clear template plastic, iron, Fray Check, nonstick pressing sheet, gluestick		

Getting It Together

1. Pin the outer and inner box fabrics, right sides together. Trace template A onto the back of the fabric.

2. Sew around the perimeter of the shape, directly on the drawn line. Leave an opening where indicated on the pattern. Clip the corners and curves. Reinforce all corners with Fray Check and let dry. (**Fig. A**)

3. Use a gluestick to tack each interfacing shape to the corresponding space on the unit from Step 2, leaving an ⅛″ margin between the interfacing shapes and the stitching. This small margin will make it easier to fold the box. Let the glue dry.

4. Place the unit, interfacing side down, onto a nonstick pressing sheet. Press with a hot iron to fuse the interfacing to the fabric. Let cool. (**Fig. B**)

5. Turn the box right side out, using a turning tool to push out the corners. Use a ladder stitch (page 10) to close the opening. Press both sides with a hot iron to fuse interfacing to both fabrics.

6. Topstitch ⅛″ around the perimeter of the entire shape. (**Fig. C**)

7. To assemble, place a gift card onto the bottom rectangle. Fold the sides in 1 at a time, tucking straight sides under curved sides. (**Fig. D**)

Done!

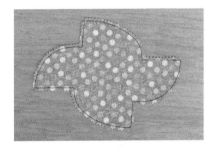
Fig. A Sewn and trimmed

Fig. B The heavy interfacing will add body to the shapes.

Fig. C Topstitched box opened flat

Fig. D Folding in the flaps is as much fun as receiving this fun gift box!

Ladder Stitch

An invisible closure for an opening, such as one left for turning and stuffing.

The Furoshiki Gift-Card Box is a beautiful, reusable alternative to traditional wrapping for gift cards.

This box features the Early Bird Newspaper Cuttings for Collage by SUCH Designs for Windham.

This box features a Japanese novelty fabric.

This box features Small Susana from the Tana Lawn collection by Liberty Fabrics.

Waterproof Patio Art

Erin Schlosser

FINISHED BANNER: 14″ × 18″

Who says that art can be seen and appreciated only indoors? Use some of your favorite fabrics and complete this no-sew project to admire on the patio all year long!

Style photography by Page + Pixel and Carly Jean Marin and instructional photography by Diane Pedersen

ERIN SCHLOSSER's love of sewing and design began in elementary school when she graphed the dimensions of her bedroom, which she then proceeded to fill with home decor projects of her own design. By high school she was teaching private sewing lessons and leading DIY projects of all sorts. After graduation, she crisscrossed the country earning degrees in interior design. Today, Erin regularly teaches a variety of workshops, guild events, and summer camps, where she never lets anyone give up on their next creative endeavor. Her work has been published in numerous design magazines, and fabric manufacturers and sewing machine companies who appreciate her clean, efficient projects frequently solicit her designs. When she's not teaching classes, Erin enjoys working with her home design clients, creating her own line of sewing patterns, cooking with her husband, and napping with the cats.

This project originally appeared in *Sew Home*, by Erin Schlosser, available from Stash Books.

- Cutting fabric for appliqué
- Using multipurpose cloth

Materials and Supplies

14" × 22" RECTANGLE OF ROC-LON
MULTIPURPOSE CLOTH

MOD PODGE OUTDOOR

16" × 24" RECTANGLE OF NEUTRAL
BACKGROUND FABRIC

TEAL AND YELLOW FABRIC SCRAPS FOR
QUOTE AND SUN CUTOUTS

POLYACRYLIC CLEAR SEALER AND
PAINTBRUSH

E6000 PERMANENT CRAFT ADHESIVE

A SHEET OF PAPER AT LEAST 11" SQUARE
FOR THE SUN PATTERN AND PRINTER
PAPER FOR THE LETTER PATTERNS

HEAVY STARCH SPRAY

BRANCH (for a more natural, outdoor
look) OR DOWEL AT LEAST 18" LONG, 1"
DIAMETER (or smaller)

Construction

1. Cover the front of the multipurpose cloth piece with the outdoor Mod Podge. Carefully affix the neutral background fabric to it. Make sure there are no creases or lumps and that everything is nice and smooth. Let it dry, then turn the piece over and fold the extra 1" of fabric to the back and secure it with more Mod Podge.

2. While the background is drying, prepare the quote and sun shape.

Cut out a 10" yellow circle. From the top of the circle, measure down from the top 4" and trim across to make the sun shape.

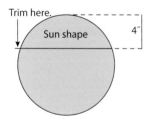

Cut various lengths and widths of small yellow strips for the sun rays from the remainder of your yellow circle. Set aside.

3. Heavily starch the fabrics for the text and set aside to dry. Use a word processing or photo-editing program to arrange the lettering. Type "This is my" and "place." Adjust the lettering height so the upper-case T is approximately 1¾" high. Print. Use the printout as a pattern to cut your shapes from the teal fabric. Then type "HAPPY" into the program. Adjust the sizing so the upper-case letters are about 2¾" high. Print. Use the printout as a pattern to cut your shapes from the yellow fabric.

4. Once the background has dried, apply another coat of outdoor Mod Podge to the top of it. This time, though, apply it a little at a time. While it's still wet, affix the letters, sun, and sun rays to it. Let it dry, then coat with another layer of outdoor Mod Podge. Once this has dried, coat with 2 layers of the polyacrylic sealer.

5. Turn the artwork over and coat the back and edges with the polyacrylic sealer. When the sealer is thoroughly dry, fold the top edge over the branch or dowel to determine how much of a fold you need. Remove the branch and put a bead of E6000 on the top edge of the back. Fold the edge down to the desired length to form a hanging sleeve and place some heavy books along the glued edge to hold it in place while the glue dries.

When the glue is dry, insert the branch or dowel into the top and hang!

tip If you have a digital die cutter, use it to cut out your fabric letters, easy-peasy!

True North Tote

Jen Fox and Sarah Case

FINISHED TOTE:
15″ wide × 14½″ high × 2″ deep

The True North Tote is an accessory that offers a lot of opportunities for personalizing with your own unique style. Try using high-contrast fabrics for a bold bag or analogous or monochromatic color schemes for a more subdued look.

Style photography by Lucy Glover and instructional photography by Diane Pedersen

JEN FOX is Jen Fox is the owner of Jen Fox Studios, an independent sewing pattern and textile design company. Armed with a background in interior design, she began the company while in design school and continues to build it while working full time designing interior spaces for a commercial architecture firm in New Mexico. When she isn't hiking, biking, and exploring the mountains and desert of the southwest, Jen can be found exploring her current city of Albuquerque, New Mexico.

WEBSITE: foxlyhandmade.com

SARAH CASE is an artist, designer, and seamstress. In 2006, she started her own jewelry line. In 2010, fueled by her Textiles and Art degree, her focus turned to a deeper passion for fabric, fibers, design, and experimentation. A love of people, travel, and adventure inspires her work. When she isn't designing, Sarah can be found biking, skiing, knitting, dancing around her kitchen while cooking, or with camera in hand exploring a new place.

This project originally appeared in *Transfer · Embellish · Stitch*, by Jen Fox and Sarah Case, available from Stash Books.

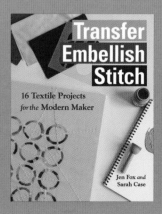

Materials

Transfer method: Embroidery tracing paper

EMBROIDERY TRACING PAPER

BALLPOINT PEN OR PENCIL

Embellishment technique: Hand embroidery

EMBROIDERY FLOSS: 3 colors of your choice, or:

   1 skein to match main body fabric

   1 skein to match contrasting body fabric

   1 skein of accent color

EMBROIDERY NEEDLE

Project

MAIN BODY FABRIC: 5/8 yard

CONTRASTING BODY FABRIC: 1/3 yard

LINING FABRIC: 3/4 yard

STRAP MATERIAL: kraft-tex (by C&T Publishing), 7/8 yard (This allows you to cut straps without piecing and is enough for 4 totes if you are making multiples.)

MEDIUM-WEIGHT WOVEN INTERFACING: 20″ wide, 2 1/4 yards (optional)

COORDINATING THREAD

MAGNETIC PURSE SNAP (*optional*)

Cutting

MAIN BODY FABRIC

TOP BAND: Cut 2 rectangles 16 1/2″ × 3 1/2″.

PANEL A: Cut 1 rectangle 8″ × 13 1/2″.

PANEL B: Cut 1 rectangle 9″ × 13 1/2″.

BACK PANEL C: Cut 1 rectangle 16 1/2″ × 13 1/2″.

CONTRASTING BODY FABRIC

REVERSE APPLIQUÉ CONTRAST: Cut 1 rectangle 8″ × 13 1/2″.

CONTRAST STRIP: Cut 1 rectangle 1 1/2″ × 13 1/2″.

LINING FABRIC

LINING BODY: Cut 2 rectangles 16 1/2″ × 16″.

INTERIOR POCKETS: Cut 2 rectangles 10″ × 7″.

INTERFACING (OPTIONAL)

EXTERIOR and LINING BODY: Cut 4 rectangles 16 1/2″ × 16″.

STRAP MATERIAL

STRAPS: Cut 4 rectangles 1″ × 26″.

HAND WASH THE KRAFT-TEX IN THE SINK. While the water is running, crinkle and crush the material to make it supple and flexible. Hang to dry.

Construction

All seam allowances are 1/2″ unless noted otherwise.

EMBELLISHMENT TECHNIQUE: REVERSE APPLIQUÉ

Make a copy of the True North motif (page 90). Follow the reverse appliqué instructions (page 19), using embroidery tracing paper (page 18) to place the motif on the wrong side of the large reverse appliqué contrast piece, as shown. Create the reverse appliqué using Panel A and the contrast piece.

Complete the reverse appliqué with a machine blanket stitch or zigzag stitch around all of the raw edges of the motif.

ASSEMBLING THE EXTERIOR BODY

1. Sew the right hand side of Panel A to one of the long sides of the contrast strip, right sides together. Press the seam toward Panel A.

2. Sew the other long side of the contrast strip to Panel B. Press the seam toward Panel B.

3. Sew one long side of one top band to the top of the A/B panel. Press the seam away from the top band.

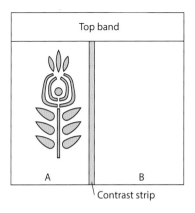

4. Sew the remaining top band to the long side of Panel C. Press the seam away from the top band.

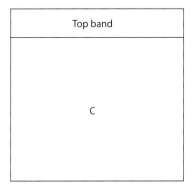

5. Follow the manufacturer's instructions to fuse an interfacing piece to the wrong side of each finished exterior piece.

EMBELLISHMENT TECHNIQUE: HAND EMBROIDERY

Now, the fun part! Using these instructions as a general guide, use the embroidery floss to create your own expression.

Stitch 3 vertical rows of hand-embroidered running stitches (page 19) on the contrast strip, using the floss that matches your main body fabric. About 1″ to the right of the contrast strip edge, use the accent embroidery floss to make a vertical running stitch from the bottom of the bag to the seam of the top band. Use a series of horizontal running stitches on the top band to create texture and interest, experimenting with adding a pop of the accent floss color to 1 or 2 rows of stitches. Knot all floss ends on the wrong side of the fabric.

MAKING THE STRAPS

1. Layer 2 kraft-tex strap pieces and clip together (pins will leave permanent holes). Sew each long side of the strap about ⅛″ from the edge. Repeat with the remaining 2 strap pieces.

2. Align the short ends of one strap with the top raw edge of an exterior body piece, approximately 3″ in from the sides, as shown. Clip and baste in place.

tip If you prefer a softer, more flexible strap, try substituting fabric straps for the kraft-tex. To create fabric straps, simply fold 2 interfaced 4″ × 26″ fabric rectangles. Sew along each long edge.

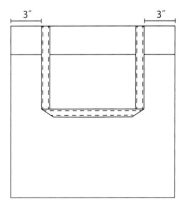

MAKING THE POCKET

1. Layer the 2 pocket pieces right sides together and pin. Stitch around the edges, but leave approximately 3″ open on one long edge (this will be the bottom of the pocket). Trim the corners, taking care not to cut into the stitching.

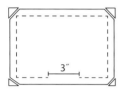

2. Turn the pocket right side out. Make sure the raw edges of the gap are on the inside of the pocket and press.

3. Topstitch the top edge of the pocket ¼″ from the edge.

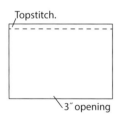

Topstitch.

3″ opening

ASSEMBLING THE INTERIOR BODY

1. Follow the manufacturer's instructions to fuse an interfacing piece to the wrong side of each lining piece.

2. Center the pocket on one lining piece, approximately 4″ above the bottom raw edge.

3. Topstitch the pocket in place along the side and bottom edges, using a ¼″ seam allowance. You may also sew several dividers in the pocket for smaller objects by sewing vertical lines on the pocket.

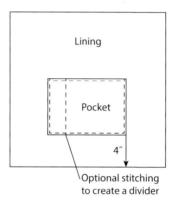

Lining

Pocket

4″

Optional stitching to create a divider

SEWING IT ALL TOGETHER

1. Pin and sew the exterior body pieces, right sides together, on the sides and bottom.

2. Pinch and pull the bag sides apart at the bottom corners and align the bottom seam with the side seam. Using a clear ruler and a rotary cutter, mark a line 1″ in from the tip, perpendicular to the seam. Sew on the line and cut away the excess. Repeat on the opposite bottom corner.

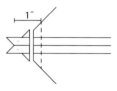

1″

3. Repeat Steps 1 and 2 with the lining pieces, except leave an opening of about 4″ at the bottom for turning.

4. Turn the lining right side out. Place the exterior inside the lining, right sides together, aligning the top edges and side seams. Carefully pin together along the top raw edge. Sew together in one continuous line around the top of the bag. If you choose, stitch over the handles a second time along the same seam line for extra strength.

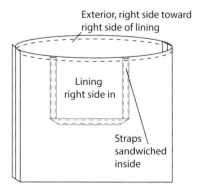

Exterior, right side toward right side of lining

Lining right side in

Straps sandwiched inside

5. Turn the bag right side out by pulling the exterior through the gap left in the lining. Push the lining back into the exterior shell.

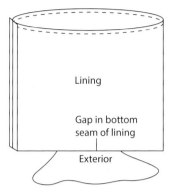

Optional Magnetic Snap

1. Measure down 1″ from the top center of the bag on each side of the lining and mark the location of the snap.

2. Trace the holes in the metal disks from the snap onto the lining fabric at the 1″ mark. With a seam ripper or small, sharp fabric scissors, cut 2 small slits through the lining/interfacing only.

3. Fit the snap prongs through the slits, and reach through the gap in the lining to place the metal disk on the slits inside the lining. Fold the prongs inward to secure. Repeat on the other side of the lining with the other half of the snap.

FINISHING

1. Press the top seam flat. Topstitch along top edge ¼″ from the finished edge.

2. Pull the lining out and pinch the fabric together at the opening, pushing the seam allowances inside. Topstitch across the gap close to the edges.

Embroidery Tracing Paper

Embroidery tracing paper is handy for transferring temporary stitching guidelines. It can be found at your local sewing shop.

Materials

- Embroidery tracing paper
- Photocopy of motif
- Ballpoint pen or pencil

1. Place the tracing paper with the colored side down on the right side of the fabric.

tip Choose a light-colored tracing paper to trace on dark fabrics and a dark-colored paper for light fabrics. Test how well the marks remove on a scrap of fabric first.

2. Position the motif, right side up, on top of the tracing paper. Tape in place. Firmly trace the motif with the ballpoint pen or pencil to transfer it to the fabric.

Running Stitch

A running stitch is the simplest, most basic embroidery stitch. It can be used to add visual interest and texture to a piece without distracting from the other elements going on in the project. This stitch can also be used for hand quilting.

Insert the threaded needle up from the back of the project at point A. Insert it back through at point B, and bring the tip up again at point C. You may be able to complete several stitches at a time, pulling the thread all the way through after a few stitches.

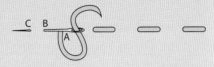

Reverse Appliqué

Reverse appliqué is a decorative sewing technique in which a motif is cut out from a top layer of fabric to expose one or more layers of fabric underneath. It can be done by hand with needle-turn appliqué, or by machine, as in the projects in this book. This technique adds depth and texture to a project.

Materials

- Fabric, main color (top layer)
- Fabric, contrasting color (bottom layer)
- Fabric, accents (optional—middle layers)
- Thread—the bobbin thread will show in this method
- Straight pins
- Appliqué scissors or small sharp fabric scissors

1. Using the design transfer method of your choice, transfer the motif to the wrong side of the contrasting fabric. (Fig. A)

NOTE: If you are using solid-colored fabrics, it is helpful to remember that the side with the transferred motif becomes the wrong side of the fabric. The side without it becomes the right side of the fabric and will be visible.

2. Lay the main-color fabric right side down. Lay the contrasting-color fabric, right side down, on top of the main-color fabric. The transferred motif should be facing up. (Fig. B)

3. Pin the layers of fabric together. Carefully sew along the traced lines with a straight stitch. (Fig. C)

Fig. A

Fig. B

Fig. C

Reverse Appliqué *continued*

4. Flip the piece over so that the right side of the main fabric is facing up. Use a small scissors to cut away the main color within the motif, revealing the contrasting reverse appliqué underneath. Pinch the top and bottom layers away from one another before poking through the top layer with the scissors to be sure to cut only the top layer. (Figs. D & E)

tip You may choose to go over the raw edges of the main-color fabric with a blanket or zigzag machine stitch. Or you may leave the edges raw for a frayed look.

Fig. D

Fig. E

Classic Insulated Lunch Bag

Virginia Lindsay

FINISHED BAG:
7½" wide × 9½" high × 5" deep
(not including tab top)

With four kids, I pack lunches almost every morning. Although I have created many lunch bag styles over the years, this one is a new favorite because it holds a lot of reusable lunch containers, closes easily at the top with hook-and-loop tabs, and has a cute classic look. If you'd like to make them to sell, lunch bags sell best in the summer and early fall. Stock up on these in June and see them sell like crazy all the way through September. Suggested price point: $18 to $25.

Fabric (for featured project): Modern Yardage's Cool Jazz, Blumen, and Burst, designed by Liz Ablashi

Styled photos by Nissa Brehmer and instructional photos by Diane Pedersen

VIRGINIA LINDSAY is is a self-taught sewist and lover of all things fabric. She is the author of a popular sewing blog and the designer behind Gingercake Patterns. Several of her patterns are published by Simplicity. Virginia lives in Freeport, Pennsylvania.

WEBSITE: gingercake.org

This project originally appeared in *Sewing to Sell—The Beginner's Guide to Starting a Craft Business*, by Virginia Lindsay, available from Stash Books.

Supplies

Quilting-weight fabric is recommended. If you are making multiples, plan your materials and cutting based on the number of items you are making to use your fabric efficiently.

1 PIECE 15½″ × 16″ MAIN EXTERIOR FABRIC (for front, back, and base)

1 PIECE 10″ × 18″ CONTRASTING EXTE-RIOR FABRIC (for sides and tab top closure)

1 PIECE 8″ × 10″ CONTRASTING FABRIC 2 (optional pocket)

1½ YARDS LIGHTWEIGHT, NONWOVEN FUSIBLE INTERFACING, 20″ wide (I use Pellon 931TD)*

1 PIECE 10″ × 32½″ LINING FABRIC

1 PIECE 10″ × 32½″ INSULATED BATTING (such as Insul-Fleece by C&T Publishing or Insul-Bright by The Warm Company)

7″ PIECE OF 1″-WIDE SEW-IN HOOK-AND-LOOP TAPE

* Interfacing is required only if using quilting-weight cotton. Laminated cotton or sturdy duck cloth would not require interfacing.

Construction

Seam allowances are ¼″ unless other-wise noted. Backstitch or lockstitch at the beginning and end of all seams.

PREPARE THE PIECES

1. Cut the fabric according to the list and the three cutting diagrams (right).

   Main exterior fabric: 2 rectangles 8″ × 10″ and 1 rectangle 5½″ × 8″

   Contrasting exterior fabric: 2 rect-angles 5½″ × 10″ and 2 rectangles 3½″ × 8″

   Lining: 2 rectangles 8″ × 10″, 2 rect-angles 5½″ × 10″, and 1 rectangle 5½″ × 8″

   Interfacing: 4 rectangles 8″ × 10″, 4 rectangles 5½″ × 10″, 2 rect-angles 5½″ × 8″, and 4 rectangles 3½″ × 8″

   Batting: 2 rectangles 8″ × 10″, 2 rectangles 5½″ × 10″, and 1 rect-angle 5½″ × 8″

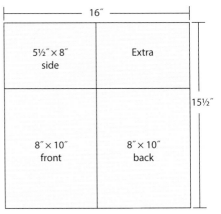

Lining fabric, batting

Main exterior fabric

tip You can fuse larger pieces of interfacing to the back of your fab-rics before cutting, and then cut the fabric and interfacing all together. What you waste in mate-rials, you may save in time.

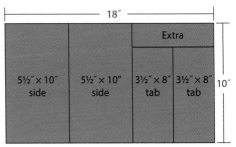

Contrast exterior fabric

2. Fuse the corresponding interfacing pieces to the back of all the quilting-weight cotton pieces.

3. Baste the batting pieces to the wrong side of the corresponding exterior pieces, using a ⅛″ seam allowance. (You can also skip the basting and just pin the exterior and batting pieces together as you go).

4. Optional: Fold the 8″ × 10″ pocket piece in half, wrong sides together, so that the folded piece is 5″ × 8″. Press and topstitch along the folded edge.

5. Fold the 3½″ × 8″ rectangles for the tab closure in half lengthwise, wrong sides together, so that the folded piece is 1¾″ × 8″. Finger-press to crease and unfold. Pin 1 piece of hook-and-loop tape to the right side of the tab, centered and ¼″ away from the fold. Sew around all 4 edges of the tape. Sew the other piece of the tape to the remaining tab the same way.

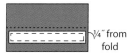

¼″ from fold

6. Refold the tabs on the center crease, right sides together. Pin and sew the short edges. Clip the corners and turn right side out. Press flat on the side *without the hook-and-loop tape.*

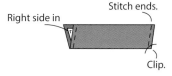

Right side in
Stitch ends.
Clip.

CONSTRUCT THE LUNCH BAG BODY

1. Using a straightedge and a pencil (or some light marking tool), mark a line on the wrong side of the 5½″ × 8″ lining base piece ¼″ in from each side. Repeat with the 5½″ × 8″ batting base piece. These lines will make it simple and accurate to sew the sides later.

Base, batting

Mark ¼″ in all sides.

2. Pin the 5½″ × 8″ exterior base piece to a 5½″ × 10″ exterior side piece, wrong sides together (in this case, batting sides together), along the short sides. Sew with the base facing up, starting and stopping your stitching line ¼″ in from the corners, using the lines drawn in Step 1.

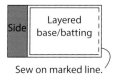

Side
Layered base/batting

Sew on marked line.

3. Repeat Step 2 to attach the other 5½″ × 10″ exterior side piece to the base.

4. Optional: Layer the pocket on top of the 8″ × 10″ exterior front piece, aligning the raw edges at the bottom and sides. Pin or baste in place.

5. Repeat Step 3 again to attach the exterior front and back pieces to the base.

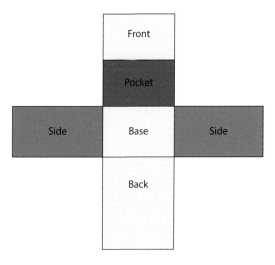

Front

Pocket

Side · Base · Side

Back

6. Fold the exterior bag from a corner of the base so the front and an adjacent side meet. Pin them right sides together and sew from the top down, again stopping ¼" short, just like with the base. Repeat this step to sew up all the side seams.

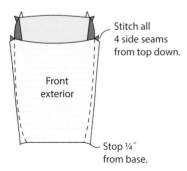

Stitch all 4 side seams from top down.

Front exterior

Stop ¼" from base.

7. Trim the seams and clip the corners. Turn the exterior bag right side out and press.

8. Repeat Steps 2–6 with the lining pieces, but make sure to leave a 4" gap in one of the lining sides so you can turn the entire piece right side out later. Clip the corners of the lining.

ATTACH THE HANDLES AND FINISH THE BAG

1. Pin the tabs to the top of the bag exterior, at the front and back, right sides together, with the hook-and-loop side of the tabs away from the bag. Baste in place with an ⅛" seam allowance.

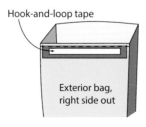

Hook-and-loop tape

Exterior bag, right side out

2. Insert the exterior bag inside the lining, right sides together, and line up the seams at the top. Pin and sew around the entire opening.

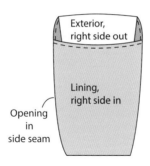

Exterior, right side out

Lining, right side in

Opening in side seam

3. Trim the seam around the top edge and then reach inside the opening left in the lining. Pull the exterior bag out and then pull the lining right side out too. Push the lining inside the exterior body.

4. Pull the lining back out and press the raw edges of the lining opening under. Either blindstitch the opening closed or topstitch it closed as close to the edge as possible. Push the lining back inside the bag.

5. Press the bag well, paying special attention to the opening.

6. Topstitch around the bag opening. Close the bag at the hook-and-loop tabs; push in the sides to make the classic lunch bag look. Iron the sides in or just fold the bag neatly and let the fabric "train" itself to naturally close with the sides in.

....

NOTE

- You can make additions to this bag, including a zippered pocket, pockets on both sides, or interior pockets.
- You can also really simplify the bag for a quick sew by having no pockets, using all one fabric, eliminating the Insul-Fleece batting, or changing the closure to a button and elastic cord. So quick and easy.
- Try appliqué, patchwork, or trim to dress up the lunch bag and show your sewing strengths.

....

Two-Bottle Tote

Janelle MacKay

FINISHED TOTE:

10″ wide × 14½″ high × 4″ deep

Made by Janelle MacKay

Whether bringing a hostess gift to the neighbors, shopping at the wine store, or going to an outdoor barbecue, I have always felt a bit uncomfortable lugging a bottle of wine or two in a crinkled brown paper bag. Not stylish! This tall, classy, and unnoticeably deceptive tote can handle two very large bottles—one for you and one for the neighbor, too. It's padded inside and has a handy divider that can easily be flipped to the side, so the bag can play double-duty as a shopping tote or large carryall.

Fabric: Tartan in Aquamarine by Joel Dewberry, FreeSpirit Fabrics

Style photography by Nissa Brehmer and instructional photography by Diane Pedersen

JANELLE MACKAY, of Emmaline Bags, designs her own line of metal bag hardware and sewing patterns. She lives in Spruce Grove, Alberta, Canada. The majority of Janelle's day is spent filling bag-bling orders, sewing bag prototypes for patterns, shoveling snow, and dreaming of warm places.

WEBSITE: emmalinebags.com

This project originally appeared in *On-the-Go Bags—15 Handmade Purses, Totes & Organizers*, by Lindsay Conner and Janelle MacKay, available from Stash Books.

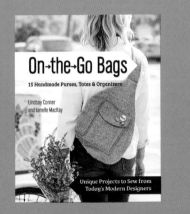

Materials and Supplies

QUILTING COTTON: 44" wide

OUTER FABRIC: ½ yard

OUTER ACCENT FABRIC: ⅓ yard (or use linen or home decor fabric)

LINING FABRIC: ½ yard

INTERFACING: 1¾ yards of 20"-wide light-to medium-weight, woven, fusible inter-facing (such as Pellon Shape-Flex SF101)

STABILIZERS:

HEAVYWEIGHT: 10" × 6" of one-sided, fusible heavyweight interfacing or stabi-lizer (such as Pellon Peltex 71F)

LIGHTWEIGHT: 1 piece of 16" × 41" lightweight stabilizer (such as ByAnnie's Soft and Stable, Automotive headliner foam, or a fusible needled fleece)

SEW-IN HOOK-AND-LOOP TAPE: 8" length

RECTANGULAR RINGS OR D-RINGS: 1" size, 2 for bag strap

STRAP BUCKLE WITH CENTER BAR AND PIN: ¾" size

MAGNETIC PURSE SNAP: ¾" size

EYELETS WITH SETTING TOOL: 2, ³⁄₁₆" size

WATER-SOLUBLE FABRIC MARKER

WALKING FOOT FOR SEWING MACHINE

Cutting

All cutting measurements are listed as width × height, unless otherwise stated.

OUTER FABRIC

Cut 2 squares 15" × 15" for external side panels.

Cut 1 rectangle 10¾" × 4¾" for external base.

Cut 2 rectangles 15" × 4" for internal facings.

Cut 2 rectangles 4¼" × 3" for strap tabs.

OUTER ACCENT FABRIC

Cut 2 strips 4" × 12" for belt straps.

Cut 1 strip 4½" × 27" for shoulder strap.

LINING FABRIC

Cut 1 rectangle 15" × 11½" for lining side A.

Cut 2 rectangles 7⅞" × 11½" for lining side B.

Cut 2 rectangles 5½" × 10" for divider.

Cut 1 rectangle 10½" × 4¾" for lining base.

INTERFACING

Interfacing pieces can be cut ½"–1" smaller than listed in order to reduce bulk in the seams.

Cut 2 squares 15" × 15" for external side panels.

Cut 2 rectangles 10¾" × 4¾" for external base (cut full size; do not reduce).

Cut 2 rectangles 15" × 4" for internal facings.

Cut 1 rectangle 15" × 11½" for lining side A.

Cut 2 rectangles 7⅞" × 11½" for lining side B.

STABILIZERS

Cut 2 squares 15" × 15" of lightweight stabilizer for external panels.

Cut 1 rectangle 5½" × 10" of lightweight stabilizer for divider.

Cut 1 rectangle 10¾" × 4¾" of lightweight stabilizer for lining base.

Cut 1 rectangle 9¾" × 4" of heavyweight stabilizer for external base.

Cut 2 squares 1½" × 1½" of heavyweight stabilizer for magnetic snap insertion.

Instructions

All seam allowances are 3/8" unless otherwise noted.

FUSE INTERFACING AND ATTACH STABILIZER

Follow the manufacturer's directions to fuse interfacing to the wrong side of the coordinating pieces.

Attach the Soft and Stable

1. With *right sides up*, place the exterior panels onto the lightweight stabilizer. Pin every few inches, around the perimeter.

2. Machine baste around the edges using a 1/4" seam allowance and a long basting stitch.

3. Carefully trim next to your basting stitches, cutting away all the stabilizer from the seam allowances.

4. Repeat Steps 1–3 for the lining base piece.

ASSEMBLE THE EXTERIOR BAG

Make the Shoulder Strap

1. Refer to 4-Fold Closed-End Strap (page 28) to make the shoulder strap.

2. Repeat the top stitching 1/8" from the first stitching line to make 2 rows of top stitching around the strap.

3. Slide a 1" metal ring onto one end and fold the end over 1 1/2". Sew a box with an X through it to secure the strap end to the strap.

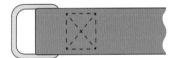

4. Repeat Step 3 for the other end of the strap.

....

NOTE: For the exterior base you will fuse one piece of the woven interfacing to the *wrong side* of the fabric piece first. Then center the fusible heavyweight stabilizer on this, and cover it with the second layer of woven interfacing. Spritz with water and use steam to press through all 4 layers. The 1 1/2" square of fusible heavyweight interfacing for the magnetic snap will be used later in the instructions.

4-Fold Straps

4-FOLD OPEN-END STRAP

Open-end straps have raw edges and are often used when the strap ends will be sewn into the seam, such as a shoulder strap or strap tabs. Use the provided measurements given in the project instructions included in this book and the following directions to make your bag strap. If you are creating a bag strap for your own project, you will need to take the desired width of the bag strap you need and multiply that by 4 to get the width of fabric required, and the length of the strap you want plus any seam allowances at the ends to get the length of fabric required.

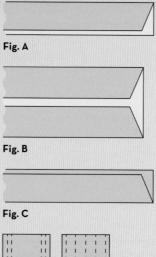

Fig. A

Fig. B

Fig. C

1. Fold the entire strap in half lengthwise with the wrong sides together and press. (Fig. A)

2. Open the strap again, fold the outside edges toward the center fold mark, and press. (Fig. B)

3. Refold the entire strip in half once again, meeting the folded edges together, and press. (Fig. C)

4. Topstitch around all 4 sides, using a long stitch length and staying about ⅛" from the edges. Continue topstitching the strap in your preferred style to match the rest of your project. (Fig. D)

Fig. D Some options for topstitching your straps

tip

• If you are using quilting cottons, you may want to add strength and a bit of structure to your bag strap. Do this by fusing a piece of light- to medium-weight interfacing in one or both of the center quarters of the strap. Cut interfacing that is a quarter or half of the width of the original fabric strip.

• If you find that the top layer is sliding when you are stitching, try pinning down the open side before you make your first stitches. Pin every 3" or so. If you have a material that is sliding quite a bit on itself, use a walking foot or wash-away double-sided tape to keep it in place.

4-FOLD CLOSED-END STRAP

Closed-end straps are most often used when the end of the bag straps will be seen, such as when bag straps are folded over a strap ring or when they are sewn to the outside exterior of a bag. In these cases, you will not want to see the raw edges on the end of a bag strap.

1. To make a 4-Fold Closed-End Strap, use the strip of fabric required in 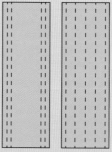 your project instructions and first press both short ends of the strap over ¼" to the wrong side of the fabric.

2. Follow 4-Fold Open-End Strap, Steps 1–4 (above), to finish making your closed-end strap.

Make the Belt

1. Refer to 4-Fold Closed-End Strap (page 28), closing only one end and leaving the other open, on one of the 12″ belt straps. Edgestitch ⅛″ from the edge on all folded edges.

2. With the strap in front of you so that the long, folded edge is on top and the seam is on the bottom, mark a placement dot on the strap 1½″ from the closed end, centered.

3. Insert one eyelet on the placement dot, following the manufacturer's directions.

4. Insert the eyelet end of the strap onto the buckle, as shown, and fold the end to the back. Pull taut and stitch across the end of the strap to secure.

5. Working on the other 12″ piece, fold back ¼″ on one of the short sides to the *wrong side* and press.

6. Fold the entire strip in half lengthwise and press.

7. To make a pointed end, open again and, working on the end that has the ¼″ pressed over, fold the outer corners toward the center fold line, creating 45° angles.

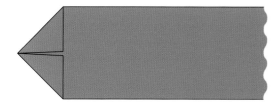

8. Trim away inside corners to reduce bulk, leaving about a ½″ seam allowance.

9. Fold the outside edges toward the center fold mark and press.

10. Refold the strip in half, meeting the folded edges together, and press.

11. Topstitch around the perimeter ⅛″ from the outer edge.

12. Working on the pointed strap, mark a placement dot on the strap 3¾″ from the point, centered.

13. Insert an eyelet on the placement dot.

14. Insert the pointed strap into the buckle of the other strap.

Assemble the Exterior Panels

1. Place the belt on the front of one of your exterior panels, with the top edge of the belt 3½" down from the top edge of the panel. Make sure the belt buckle is perfectly centered. Pin in place.

2. Baste in place in the left and right side seam allowances.

3. Anchor the belt in place by topstitching vertical lines on each strap about 1½" on either side of the belt buckle.

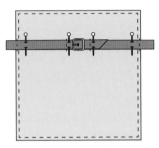

4. Trim off the belt ends so they are even with the side edges.

5. Place the exterior panels together, *right sides together*, and sew the side seams, leaving the top and bottom open. Using a pressing cloth and a warm iron, press the side seams open.

Attach the Base

1. Mark start/stop lines ³⁄₈" in from all 4 corners on the *wrong side* of the exterior base. Measure and mark the center of each side on the exterior base, as well as the top and bottom edges on the exterior side panels.

2. With *right sides together*, place one long side of the base along the bottom edge of one exterior panel, match the center marks, and pin together.

3. Stitch from the start/stop markings at one corner to the start/stop markings at the end, making sure to not sew past these marks.

4. Repeat for the other side.

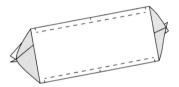

5. Center each side seam of the exterior panel on a short end of the base and pin in place. Make a small clip in the seam allowance of the side panel where the corner will be. Sew across the end of the base from edge to edge. Repeat for the other side.

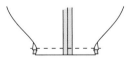

Make and Attach the Strap Tabs

1. Refer to 4-Fold Open-End Strap (page 28) to create 2 small tabs from the 2 strap tab rectangles.

NOTE: The 4¼" measurement is the width and the 3" measurement is the length.

2. Repeat the top stitching ⅛″ from the first stitching line to make 2 rows of top stitching to match the shoulder strap.

3. Slide 1 strap tab onto 1 metal ring that is attached to the shoulder strap and baste the ends closed using a ⅛″ seam allowance. Repeat with the other strap tab.

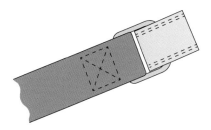

4. Center the strap tabs over the *right side* of the exterior bag side seams, matching raw edges, and pin to secure. Baste the strap tabs in place using a ¼″ seam allowance.

ASSEMBLE THE LINING

Make the Divider

1. Using a ¼″ seam allowance, baste the lightweight stabilizer onto the wrong side of 1 fabric divider piece.

2. Place the 2 divider pieces together, *right sides together*, pin, and stitch around both short ends and one long side, leaving one long side open for turning.

3. Clip the corners, trim the seam allowances to ⅛″, and turn the divider *right side out*. Press.

4. Topstitch around the sewn sides ⅛″ from the edge.

5. Sew a vertical line of stitching, lengthwise on the divider, 1″ from the side without raw edges. Then stitch another line ⅛″ on the other side of that (1⅛″ from the edge) to make 2 lines side by side.

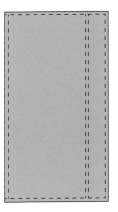

6. Center the divider between the 2 lining side B pieces. *Right sides* should be facing together and the raw edges on the sides of all 3 pieces should be aligned. Stitch through all layers to create 1 side panel with the divider flap protruding from the center. Press the seam open.

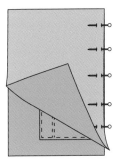

Attach the Hook-and-Loop Tape

1. Fold the lining side A piece in half crosswise and finger press to make a fold line. Unfold *right side up* and place the loop side of the hook-and-loop tape on the left side of the fold line, centered from top to bottom, and stitch in place.

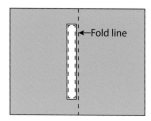

2. With the lining side B in front of you, fold the center divider to the right and place the hook side of the tape in the 1″ section on the right edge of the divider. Center it from top to bottom, and stitch in place.

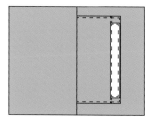

Attach the Magnetic Snap

Attach 1 magnetic snap (following manufacturers instructions) side to the center of each of the internal facing pieces.

Assemble the Lining

1. Sew 1 facing piece to the top of each lining panel. Press the seams toward the facing and topstitch on the facing side of the seam.

NOTE: The top of the side panel with the divider attached will be top edge when viewing it in the illustration in Attach the Hook-and-Loop Tape (left). The divider is flipped to the right, and the tape is on the front right of the divider.

2. Place the lining panels together, *right sides together*, and stitch the side seams, leaving an opening of 7″ on one side for turning. Press the side seams open.

3. Refer to Attach the Base (page 30) to attach the lining base.

4. To reinforce stitches and reduce bulk, after the base is attached, sew an extra round of stitching around the perimeter, stitching 1/8″ away from the first line. Trim corners and seam allowances to 1/8″.

ATTACH EXTERIOR TO LINING

1. With the lining *wrong side out* and the bag exterior *right side* out, slide the bag exterior into the lining. Match the side seams and centers and pin around the bag opening.

2. Using a 3/8″ seam allowance, sew around the bag opening. Turn the bag *right side out* using the turning hole in the lining. Sew the lining hole closed by machine with a 1/16″ seam allowance or use an invisible slip stitch by hand. Push the lining down inside the bag exterior.

3. Press the seam around the bag opening and topstitch around the bag opening to finish.

Red Stapler Pillow

Samarra Khaja

FINISHED PILLOW: 14″ × 14″

Staplers are beautiful things. They are used for furniture manufacturing, carpet tacking, insulation and electrical wire installation, picture frame manufacturing, stitching in medical fields, and of course home/office use. Who knew one tiny bent piece of metal could afford us with so many options in life? Because something so seemingly mundane does so much for us, it only makes sense to give it a wink and shout-out. Hello, throw pillow. Yes, I know I read your mind on that one. Not to worry, ducklings, we are one here, and we both know a red stapler pillow is the next necessary addition to any self-respecting household. So let's get to it.

Style photography by Nissa Brehmer and instructional photography by Diane Pedersen

NOTE: FUN FACTS

Swingline. Office Space. Need I say more? If you know the movie, you know all about red Swingline staplers. But did you know that none existed before the movie came out in 1999? A handful were sprayed red at an auto body paint shop for prop use in the movie. When people saw the beautiful specimens twinkling on the big screen, they barraged Swingline with requests for red staplers. In 2002, the company obliged. Since then, all has been right in the land.

SAMARRA KHAJA is an illustrator, graphic designer, and award-winning author of *Sew Adorkable: 15 DIY Projects to Keep You Out of Trouble, Off the Bookshelf*, and *Off the Beaten Path.*

WEBSITE: samarrakhaja.com

This project originally appeared in *Sew Adorkable*, by Samarra Khaja, available from Stash Books.

What You'll Need

Red Stapler patterns (page 91)

TURQUOISE FABRIC: 1 square 15" × 15" for pillow front

RED FABRIC: For stapler body

ORANGE FABRIC: For stapler highlights

GRAY FABRIC: For stapler accents

DARK PRINT FABRIC: For stapler base

SAMARRA'S SCHOOL SUPPLIES FABRIC: For pillow back—Cut 1 square 15" × 15".

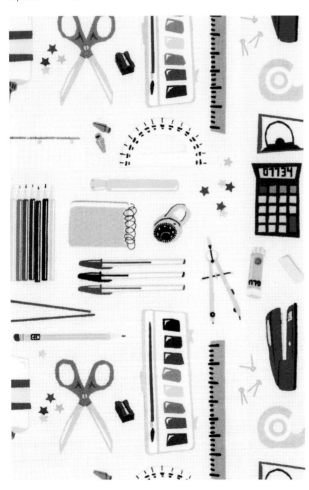

STRIPED FABRIC AND PIPING CORD (OPTIONAL): For piping

METALLIC SILVER THREAD: For accents

PAPER-BACKED FUSIBLE WEBBING

PILLOW INSERT: 14" × 14"

It's Go Time

Seam allowances are ½" for this project.

1. Trace all pattern pieces onto paper-backed fusible webbing, leaving extra paper around each piece. Note that the patterns are in reverse so that the pieces will be oriented correctly for fusing (Steps 4 and 5). Refer to the stapler assembly diagram (below) as a cutting guide.

2. Iron each loosely cut piece to the back of its corresponding fabric; fuse in place.

3. Cut out all stapler pieces along the pencil lines, cutting through the paper and fabric layers.

4. Place the pillow background fabric flat on the ironing board, and position all stapler pieces into the center area of the fabric square, using the pattern as your guide.

5. Iron to fuse all the layers together. Tack first, if necessary, to ensure that the pieces don't shift before they're permanently secured.

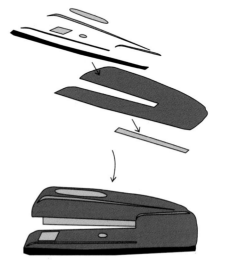

All Together Now

1. Use metallic silver embroidery thread to hand embroider the remaining stapler accents.

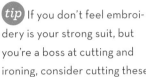

tip If you don't feel embroidery is your strong suit, but you're a boss at cutting and ironing, consider cutting these last remaining stapler details out of additional fabric with paper-backed fusible and ironing them into place.

2. Topstitch around all raw appliqué areas for a finished look. I used a zigzag stitch. You may choose to use a hand-sewn finishing stitch—perhaps blanket, chain, or other fun embroidery stitch.

Almost Done!

tip If you want to add more fun to your pillow like I did, add piping or another trim, or, hello, can you go wrong with pompoms!?! If you like that idea, sandwich them in between the pillow panels as part of Step 1, so you can sew it all together in one shot. Use your own tried-and-true method for joining the piping ends.

1. Place the appliquéd pillow front and back fabric together, face to face, aligning all edges. Pin in place. (Remember, piping is optional here.)

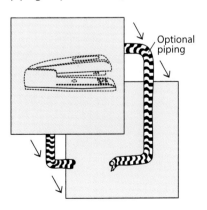

Optional piping

2. Starting along the bottom edge, sew all the way around the pillow cover, leaving a 5″ centered opening on one side for turning the pillow right side out.

tip If you suffer from throw pillow commitment phobia (TPCP) and insist on removable pillow covers, by all means go for it, using your favorite technique for inserting a zipper.

3. Trim off excess fabric at the corners, flip the pillow right side out, and iron flat. Slipstitch the opening closed.

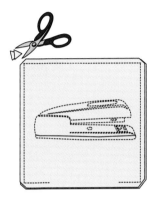

4. Insert the pillow form into the cover and hand sew the opening shut.

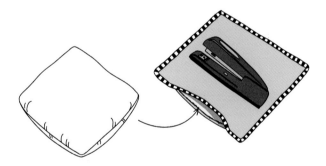

tip Sure, this appliqué looks divine as a throw pillow, but why stop there? Consider making multiples and turning it into a quilt top! My recommendation would be to make a bunch of gray stapler blocks and one lone red stapler block to make an awesome quilt!

Baby Love Large Block Quilt

Camille Roskelley

FINISHED QUILT: 36″ × 36″
FINISHED BLOCK: 30″ × 30″

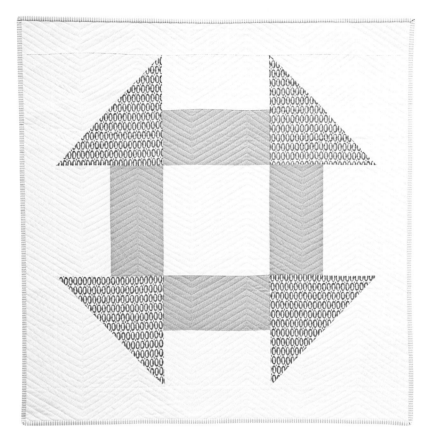

Fabric: Pezzy Print by American Jane for Moda, and Ruby by Bonnie and Camille for Moda

Flat quilt photography by Christina Carty-Francis and Diane Pedersen of C&T Publishing, Inc.; style photography by Camille Roskelley

 CAMILLE ROSKELLEY has been sewing since before she can remember, and found her love of quilting early in life. She started her pattern company Thimble Blossoms back in 2007 and began designing fabric with her mother, Bonnie, for Moda in 2008.

WEBSITE: thimbleblossoms.com

This project originally appeared in *Simply Retro with Camille Roskelley,* available from Stash Books.

Materials

Yardages are based on 42″-wide fabric.

⅓ YARD OF SOLID FABRIC for the block

⅓ YARD OF COORDINATING PRINT FABRIC for the block

1¼ YARDS OF WHITE FABRIC for the block and border

1¼ YARDS OF FABRIC for the backing

⅓ YARD OF FABRIC for the binding

40″ × 40″ PIECE OF COTTON BATTING

Cutting

FROM SOLID FABRIC: Cut 4 pieces 5½″ × 10½″.

FROM COORDINATING PRINT FABRIC: Cut 2 squares 10⅞″ × 10⅞″.

FROM WHITE FABRIC:

Cut 2 squares 10⅞″ × 10⅞″.

Cut 4 pieces 5½″ × 10½″.

Cut 1 square 10½″ × 10½″.

Cut 4 strips 3½″ × WOF* for the border.

FROM BINDING FABRIC: Cut 4 strips 2½″ × WOF.

* WOF = width of fabric

Quilt Assembly

This quilt top is a single large block. It is made up of 1 white square 10½" × 10½", 4 matching units 10½" × 10½", and 4 matching HSTs.

1. Sew 1 solid fabric piece 5½" × 10½" to 1 white piece 5½" × 10½" to make 1 unit 10½" × 10½". Press. Repeat to make a total of 4 matching units.

2. Place 1 coordinating print square 10⅞" × 10⅞" on top of 1 white square 10⅞" × 10⅞", right sides together. Make 2 HSTs. For directions, see Easy HSTs (page 38). Repeat with another set of squares to make a total of 4 matching HSTs. Press. At this point, the HSTs should measure 10½" × 10½".

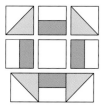

Block assembly

3. Sew together 3 rows of 3. Press. Sew the rows together to make 1 large block. Press.

4. For the border, measure your quilt and use your favorite method for sewing squared borders.

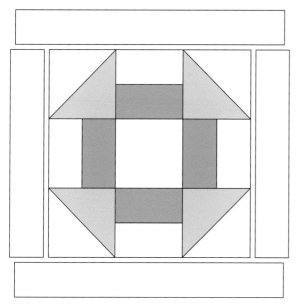

Quilt assembly

Finishing

Layer the quilt top, batting, and backing, and pin baste to make a quilt sandwich. Machine or hand quilt as desired. Bind your quilt.

tip Quilting Play

With small baby quilts, you can have fun experimenting with different quilting techniques. When I was quilting these, I used two quilting styles I hadn't ever tried. On the small blocks quilt, I stitched scallops. For the large block quilt, I did straight-line quilting in an allover zigzag pattern that added a modern touch. I loved the results!

Easy HSTs

Half-square triangles (HSTs) are super easy to make. Here's the method.

An HST is made with 2 contrasting squares of the same size. Place 1 square on top of the other with right sides together (A). On the back of the lighter square, draw a pencil line from one corner to the opposite corner (B). Sew ¼" from the line on each side (C). Cut on the line to make 2 HSTs (D). Press toward the darker of the 2 fabrics. Presto!

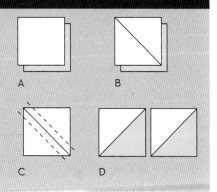

Big Pennant Quilt

Barbara Cain

FINISHED QUILTS:
Lap size: 45″ × 60″
Twin size: 60″ × 90″

The pennants that make this festive quilt are just simple, elongated isosceles triangles. They are sizable—15″ wide and 30″ long when finished—and are by far the largest component of all the quilts in this book. That makes Big Pennant super fast to put together. If you're tight on time, you might want to try this one.

Big Pennant lap-size quilt—Circus palette, made by Barbara Cain

Style photography by Nissa Brehmer and instructional photography by Diane Pedersen

BARBARA CAIN When Barbara was a young girl, her mother taught her how to sew clothing. After Barbara understood garment making, her interests quickly turned to home goods. She began making kitchen linens, decorative pillows, bedding, and, most importantly, quilts! Barbara had an undying interest in all things textile, which inspired her to pursue an education in interior design. This was followed by a long career as a partner of an architectural firm where she honed her design skills.

Due to the demands of her occupation, quilting had been a luxury hobby in Barbara's limited free time. She recognized her need to continue making quilts, but without the huge time commitment that many quilts take. This need resulted in her developing Big Bold Modern Quilts, where Barbara shares her expertise in creating large scale, sizable quilts with rewarding speed.

BLOG: modernquiltingbyb.com

This project originally appeared in *Go Big, Go Bold—Large-Scale Modern Quilts*, by Barbara Cain, available from Stash Books.

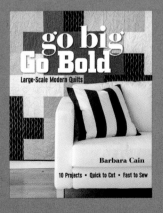

Fabrics

Big Pennant is made with three colorful fabrics and one neutral background fabric. Solids and prints work just fine for this quilt; however, when using prints, be sure to use either nondirectional or two-way directional designs.

The quilt back is made of a pennant feature section that is constructed in the same way as the quilt top. Fabric panels are situated on both sides of this feature and complete the back.

The pictured *Big Pennant* uses the Circus palette. This vivid scheme is quite playful and will certainly bring a cheerful atmosphere to any space.

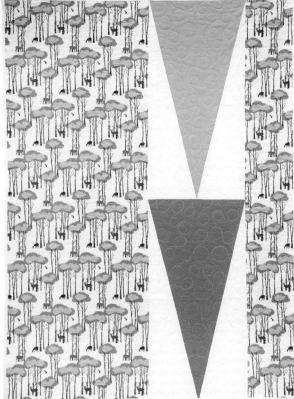

Big Pennant lap-size quilt back

Materials

Yardages are based on 40"-wide fabric.

Material	Description	Lap quilt (45" × 60")	Twin quilt (60" × 90")
Fabric 1	Chartreuse solid for the pennants	1 yard	1½ yards
Fabric 2	Jade solid for the pennants	⅞ yard	1½ yards
Fabric 3	Orange solid for the pennants	1 yard	1½ yards
Fabric 4	White print for the background	2¼ yards	3⅝ yards
Fabric 5	Multicolored print for the back panels	2 yards	4¼ yards*
Fabric 6	White solid for the binding	½ yard	¾ yard
Batting		53" × 68"	68" × 98"
Template material	Mat board, poster board, or heavy cardboard	36" × 36"	36" × 36"

* The narrower back panel requires piecing. To avoid piecing, you'll need 5⅝ yards.

Cutting

Cut all of the triangles on the crosswise grain of the fabric.

IMPORTANT! Starch your fabric before cutting triangles.

Material	Lap quilt (45" × 60")	Twin quilt (60" × 90")
Fabric 1	Cut 2 a triangles (1a).	Cut 4 a triangles (1a).
	Cut 1 f extended triangle (1f).	Cut 1 f extended triangle (1f).
Fabric 2	Cut 2 a triangles (2a).	Cut 5 a triangles (2a).
Fabric 3	Cut 3 a triangles (3a).	Cut 5 a triangles (3a).
Fabric 4	Cut 4 a triangles (4a).	Cut 9 a triangles (4a).
	Cut 3 b edge triangles (4b).	Cut 5 b edge triangles (4b).
	Cut 3 c edge triangles (4c).	Cut 5 c edge triangles (4c).
	Cut 1 d extended edge triangle (4d).	Cut 1 d extended edge triangle (4d).
	Cut 1 e extended edge triangle (4e).	Cut 1 e extended edge triangle (4e).
Fabric 5	Cut 1 piece 26¾" × 68" (5g).	Cut 1 piece 34¼" × 98" (5i).
	Cut 1 piece 11¾" × 68" (5h).	Cut 2 pieces 19¼" × 49¼" (5j).*
Fabric 6	Cut 6 strips 2½" × width of fabric for binding.	Cut 9 strips 2½" × width of fabric for binding.

* Carefully cut the fabric so that the print will match when the pieces are joined. OR if you have 5⅝ yards, cut 1 piece 19¼" × 98" (5j).

Make Templates

Refer to Making and Using Templates below.

Make templates for the a triangle, the b/c edge triangle, the d/e extended edge triangle, and the f extended triangle, as shown.

tip *Piecing Template Boards*
If you don't have access to mat board or poster board large enough for these templates, use two smaller boards and tape them together.

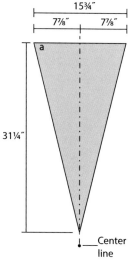

Dimensions for a triangle

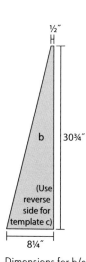

Dimensions for b/c edge triangle

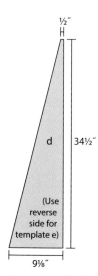

Dimensions for d/e extended edge triangle

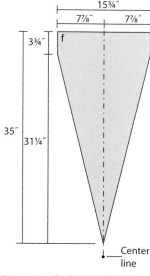

Dimensions for f extended triangle

Making and Using Templates

You will need to make cutting templates for projects that are based on triangles. You can use the same templates for both the lap- and the twin-size quilts for each design.

1. Referring to the dimensions given in the project, use a ruler, square, and permanent marker to draw each of the templates onto mat board, poster board, or heavy cardboard.

2. Depending on your level of confidence with rotary-cutting tools and the thickness of the template material you are using, cut along the drawn lines with a rotary cutter, craft knife, or box cutter, along with a ruler and cutting mat. If your template material is thin enough, you can cut with scissors.

3. Trace around the template onto the right side of the appropriate fabric. Make the most efficient use of your fabric by rotating the template when tracing.

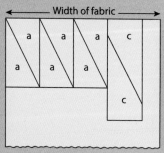

Alternate triangles for efficient use of fabric.

4. Place the fabric on a cutting mat and use a ruler and rotary cutter to cut along the traced lines to cut the individual pieces. For quilts that require the same cuts from 2 or more fabrics, you can cut more than one piece at a time by layering the fabrics, keeping the marked fabric on top, and then cutting through the stack. To maintain accuracy when cutting, it's best to limit the stack to 3 layers of fabric.

Construction

Big Pennant is assembled in triangular pairs that are further assembled into rows that form the quilt top. For the quilt back, the pairs are assembled into blocks and then into a column. All seam allowances are ¼" and are pressed to one side. When sewing the triangle pairs, press the seams toward the pennant fabric; when joining the pairs into rows, press the seams toward the background. Between rows and columns, press all the seams in one direction.

TRIANGLE PAIRS

To ensure proper alignment of triangle pairs, carefully refer to the assembly diagrams that follow.

Triangle to Triangle

1. With right sides up, place the triangles to be paired side by side. Flip one triangle onto the other along the edge to be sewn.

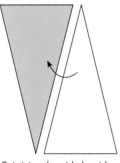

Pair triangles side by side.

2. Keeping the edges to be sewn aligned, slightly shift the pieces so that the lower pennant triangle extends beyond the upper, until the lower triangle, the upper triangle, and the ¼" seamline all intersect at the same point. Gently pin and sew together the pieces using a ¼" seam. Press seams toward the pennant fabric.

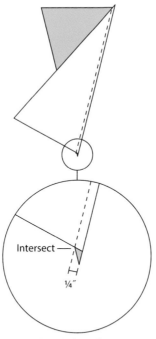

Intersect

¼"

Align, shift, and sew.

Edge Triangle to Triangle

In a manner similar to Triangle to Triangle (left), sew together the pieces as shown.

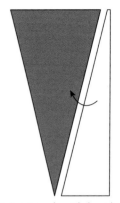

1. Pair triangles side by side.

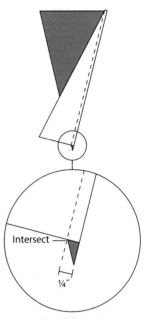

Intersect

¼"

2. Align, shift, and sew.

Extended Edge Triangle to Triangle

1. With right sides up, place pennant triangle a and extended edge triangle 4d side by side. Flip 4d onto the a triangle along the edge to be sewn.

2. Keeping the edges to be sewn aligned, slightly shift the pieces so that a extends beyond 4d, until a, 4d, and the ¼" seamline all intersect at the same point. Gently pin and sew the ¼" seam.

3. Flip 4d to its face-up position and press the seam allowance toward the pennant fabric. Trim off the protruding portion of 4d.

4. Repeat Steps 1 and 2 to add piece 4e to the 3a/4d or 2a/4d assembly. Flip 4e to its face-up position and press toward the background.

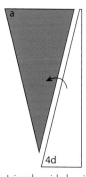

Pair triangles side by side.

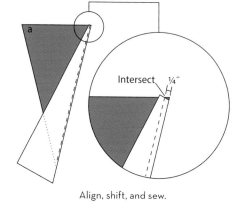

Align, shift, and sew.

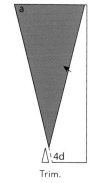

Trim.

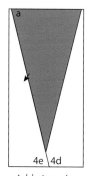

Add piece 4e.

QUILT TOP

Refer to either the lap-size quilt assembly diagram or the twin-size quilt assembly diagram.

1. Sew together the pairs into rows and press toward the background.

2. If any stretching has occurred, trim the edge triangles as needed to align with the center triangles; the pennant rows should measure 30½" high. This consists of 30¼" from the center of the pennant base to its opposite point, plus a ¼" seam allowance above the point. Trim any dog-ear triangles that extend into the seam allowances.

3. Sew together the rows to assemble the quilt top and press.

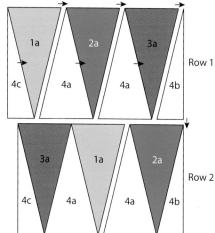

Lap-size quilt top assembly

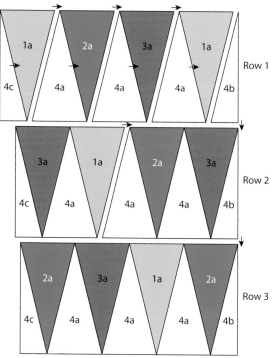

Twin-size quilt top assembly

QUILT BACK

Refer to either the lap-size quilt back assembly diagram or the twin-size quilt back assembly diagram.

1. Sew together the triangles into blocks and press. Note: If you are piecing the back panel for the twin-size quilt, match the print pattern of the 5j pieces.

2. Sew together the blocks into a column and press.

3. Sew together the columns to assemble the quilt back and press.

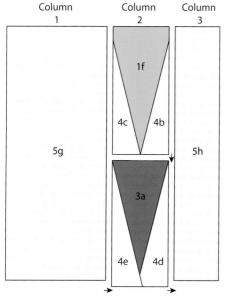

Lap-size quilt back assembly

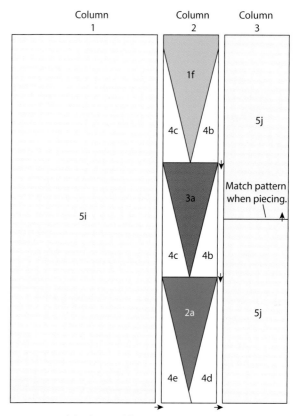

Twin-size quilt back assembly

FINISHING

Layer, quilt, and bind as desired.

Chevron Table Set

Heidi Staples

FINISHED TABLE RUNNER: 9″ × 37″
FINISHED PLACE MAT: 12″ × 17″

Chevrons are not only a great modern accent on these table items, but they also give you the chance to showcase some of your favorite prints. I chose to use a brown sketch print that has the appearance of linen without the stretchy texture that could make these Flying Geese a little more challenging to sew. One of the place mats is intended for a child, while the other three use the same prints found in the runner.

Styled photography by Nissa Brehmer and instructional photography by Diane Pedersen

HEIDI STAPLES spent ten years working in education before becoming a full-time mom. She sewed her first quilt in 2011 and was instantly hooked. Heidi lives in Fair Oaks Ranch, Texas, with her family.

WEBSITE: fabricmutt.blogspot.com

This project originally appeared in *Sew Organized for the Busy Girl*, by Heidi Staples, available from Stash Books.

CHEVRON TABLE RUNNER

9″ × 37″, featuring Sketch by Timeless Treasures Fabrics

Table Runner Materials and Cutting

Though the materials list gives you a little leeway for cutting mistakes, you can actually make these chevrons using only a stack of charm squares if you make each cut perfectly!

Fabric	For	Cutting
⅝ yard brown print	Flying Geese blocks	Cut 1 rectangle 2½″ × 4½″. Cut 2 squares 2½″ × 2½″.
	Borders	Cut 2 rectangles 3″ × 32½″. Cut 2 rectangles 3″ × 9½″.
	Binding	Cut 3 strips 2½″ × width of fabric.
Scraps at least 5″ square from 15 prints	Flying Geese blocks	From each print: Cut 1 rectangle 2½″ × 4½″. Cut 2 squares 2½″ × 2½″.
½ yard batting	Quilting	Cut 1 rectangle 15″ × 40″.
½ yard floral print	Backing	Cut 1 rectangle 15″ × 40″.

Making the Table Runner

Seam allowances are ¼″ unless otherwise noted.

FLYING GEESE BLOCKS

1. Arrange the chevron prints (2 squares and 1 rectangle each) in order.

2. Use a pencil to draw a diagonal line from corner to corner on the wrong side of each 2½″ square, including the background squares.

3. To make the first Flying Geese block, start at the top of the chevron. Pair the 2½″ background squares with the top print rectangle.

Right sides together, place a square on the left corner of the rectangle. Sew directly on the diagonal line. Trim the seam allowance to ¼″. Press the brown triangle toward the corner.

Repeat this step with the other brown square on the right side of the rectangle.

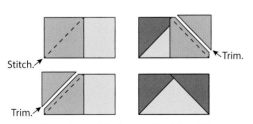

Stitch. Trim. Trim.

Flying Geese block assembly—Make 15.

4. Repeat Step 3 using the 2½″ squares from the first fabric with the rectangle from the second fabric in line. Continue making Flying Geese blocks in this fashion. The last block will combine the last 2 print squares with the brown rectangle.

TABLE RUNNER ASSEMBLY

1. Sew the Flying Geese together in 4 groups of 3 and 1 group of 4, and then sew the groups together. This will help keep the rows straight.

Sew together a row of Flying Geese.

2. Sew the 3″ × 32½″ borders to the long sides of the chevron strip. Sew the 3″ × 9½″ borders to the short ends.

FINISHING

1. Layer the backing (right side down), batting, and runner top (right side up).

2. Quilt and bind as desired.

CHEVRON PLACE MATS

12" × 17"

Place Mat Materials and Cutting

Though the materials list gives you a little leeway for cutting mistakes, you can actually make these chevrons using only a stack of charm squares if you make each cut perfectly!

Fabric	For	Cutting
½ yard brown print	Flying Geese blocks and background	Cut 3 rectangles 2½" × 4½". Cut 2 squares 2½" × 2½". Cut 1 rectangle 3½" × 12½". Cut 1 rectangle 10½" × 12½".
	Binding	Cut 2 strips 2½" × width of fabric.
Scraps at least 5" square from 3 different prints	Flying Geese blocks	From each of the 3 prints: Cut 1 rectangle 2½" × 4½". Cut 2 squares 2½" × 2½".
½ yard floral print	Backing	Cut 1 rectangle 13" × 18".
Fat quarter batting	Quilting	Cut 1 rectangle 13" × 18".

Making the Place Mat

Seam allowances are ¼" unless otherwise noted.

1. See Making the Table Runner (page 47) for instructions on making the Flying Geese blocks in a chevron pattern.

2. Sew a 2½" × 4½" brown rectangle to the top and bottom of the row.

3. Place the chevron row so that the chevrons point up. Sew the 3½" × 12½" brown rectangle to the left side of the row and the 10½" × 12½" rectangle to the right side.

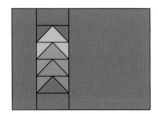

Place mat assembly

4. To finish, trim the place mat to 12½" × 17½". Use the same quilting and binding method you used for the runner. (See Finishing, page 47.)

Linen Table Runner

Kirstyn Cogan

This appliquéd table runner will be a fresh addition to any urban kitchen.

Style Photography by Nissa Brehmer; instructional photography by Diane Pedersen

KIRSTYN COGAN designs embroidery, appliqué, and surface prints for the garment industry, as well as greeting cards, stationery, and quilting fabric. Kirstyn's mission is to design and produce quality, Scandinavian-inspired products. Her studio is located in Seattle, Washington.

This project originally appeared in *Urban Scandinavian Sewing*, by Kirstyn Cogan, available as an eBook from Stash Books.

Materials

PANEL A: ½ yard linen or linen/cotton-blend fabric

PANELS B AND C: 1 fat quarter or ¼ yard contrasting linen or linen/cotton-blend fabric

COORDINATING APPLIQUÉ FABRIC: 1 fat quarter or ¼ yard (Use 1 fabric or a combination. You will have extra fabric left over.)

IRON-ON ADHESIVE: ½ yard (I used HeatnBond Feather Lite.)

FINE-TIP PERMANENT MARKER

FABRIC-MARKING PEN: Always test on a scrap of fabric before using. I recommend using FriXion pens.

ALL-PURPOSE SEWING THREAD:

To coordinate with panel A fabric

To coordinate with contrasting fabric(s)

CONTRASTING EMBROIDERY FLOSS: 1 skein

EMBROIDERY FLOSS THREADER AND NEEDLE

Optional but Helpful

ROTARY CUTTER, clear Omnigrid ruler, and self-healing cutting mat

SEAM GAUGE

Cutting

Wash, dry, and press the fabric before you cut it.

PANEL A: 14″ × 31½″

PANEL B: 1¾″ × 14″

PANEL C: 14″ × 16¾″

APPLIQUÉ FABRIC: 10″ × 14″

Make It

Use a ¼″ seam allowance unless otherwise noted.

PIECE IT

tip Make sure you've got the stitch settings for your machine just right by testing them on scrap fabric before starting on the actual project.

Panels A, B, and C placement

1. Following the placement diagram above, pin the panels together with right sides facing. Sew the 3 panels together using a straight stitch. Press the seams open.

2. Zigzag stitch over the raw edge of each back seam. Your top and bobbin thread should match the fabric you are sewing on.

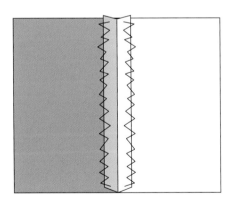

APPLIQUÉ IT

1. Enlarge the circular appliqué pattern (page 92) by 200% and then use a permanent marker to trace it onto the paper side of the iron-on adhesive and then cut out the paper rectangle (do not cut out the circles within it just yet). No need to draw the dashed line.

2. Repeat Step 1 to create a second set of appliqués. Draw the dashed line running through the circles on this set.

3. Place the appliqué fabrics right side down on the ironing board. Place both iron-on adhesive sheets on top, paper side up. Make sure the fabric is slightly larger than the paper template. Use a pressing cloth to avoid getting adhesive and ink on your iron. Following the manufacturer's instructions, press the adhesive onto the fabric.

4. Cut out the first set of appliqué shapes, including the inner circles.

5. For the second set of appliqués, cut along the dashed line to remove the side without the numbers. Then cut the curves of the circles.

6. Referring to the placement diagram, place the panel A and panel C appliqués adhesive side down on the front side of the table runner. Be sure the panel A appliqués are aligned with the raw edge of the panel fabric and the panel C appliqués begin about ½″ from the short end. Press the appliqués into place like you did in Step 3.

7. Use a zigzag stitch with thread to match the appliqué fabric to stitch the appliqués onto the table runner.

Finishing Zigzag Stitches

Thread any loose ends of thread on your hand-sewing needle and bring them to the back side. Tie a knot and then run the thread ends through several of the zigzag stitches on the back.

Finish It

1. Finish the raw edges of the runner by folding each raw edge under, wrong sides together, ¼" and pressing. Fold each side under another ¼" and press again, pinning as you go. Use a straight stitch to topstitch the folded edges down.

2. Gently make a dotted line up the center of the appliqué circles on panel C using a ruler and fabric-marking pen.

3. Tie a knot at the end of a 45" length of embroidery floss (do not separate the strands; use it as it comes off the skein), leaving a 3" tail. Come up from the back of the runner and embroider a running stitch up the line made in Step 2. Refer to the diagram for Running Stitch (page 19) as needed.

4. On the back of the runner, tie a knot at the end of the floss. Similar to the way the zigzag stitches were finished, you can thread the loose ends of embroidery floss and pull them into the hidden fold of the edge seam. Trim the ends close to the fabric and you'll never know they're there!

Tea Mat

Minki Kim

We love tea mats. They are the perfect size for a cup of tea or coffee and a little sweet treat. They are quick to sew up and make perfect gifts. Tea mats give your home a cozy, handmade look and just may inspire you to bake up a batch of scones and invite a friend over for a cup of tea and a chat.

Designed and made by Minki Kim

Style photography by Page + Pixel and instructional photography by Diane Pedersen

Materials and Supplies

For 1 tea mat.

NEUTRAL COTTON OR LINEN, COTTON PRINTS, AND COTTON BATTING: Scraps (see Cutting for sizes)

FUSIBLE WEB: Such as Steam-A-Seam

FABRIC MARKER: Frixion pen or water-soluble marker

MACHINE SEWING THREAD: Neutral (white or ivory) for piecing and dark 40-weight for outlining

HAND-EMBROIDERY THREAD: 1 color to contrast with cotton front

HAND-SEWING NEEDLES: Regular and embroidery

Cutting

NEUTRAL COTTON: 1 piece 6½″ × 9″ for front

COTTON PRINT: 1 piece 6½″ × 9″ for back

BATTING: 1 piece 6½″ × 9″

MINKI KIM is a formally trained artist and self-taught sewist. She started sewing as a creative outlet when her children were small; she wanted to capture the beauty of ordinary moments, first with hand embroidery and later by recreating them with her sewing machine and fabric–literally drawing with thread. Originally from Korea, Minki now calls Southern California home, where she lives with her husband and three young daughters.

BLOG: minkikim.com

This project originally appeared in *Sew Illustrated—35 Charming Fabric & Thread Designs*, by Minki Kim and Kristin Esser, available from Stash Books.

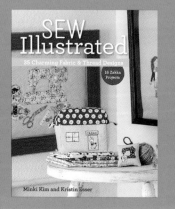

Instructions

Seam allowances are ¼" unless otherwise noted.

SEWING ILLUSTRATION

1. Transfer one of the Tea Mat designs (page 92) to the print fabric scraps. Refer to the package for instructions on how to use your brand of fusible web. (Fig. A)

2. Cut the fabric accents out on the traced lines.

3. Fuse the accents to the front fabric piece. (Fig. B)

4. Sketch in the details of the design, such as the string and front rim of the saucer.

5. Layer the tea mat top onto the batting. If you used fusible web to attach the teacups, you do not need to secure the accents with stitching. If you didn't use fusible web, secure each accent shape by stitching about ⅛" away from the edge with neutral-color thread and a stitch length of 1.6. Use an open-toe appliqué foot if you have one.

6. Thread the sewing machine with dark thread and set the stitch length to 1.6. Stitch around the edge of the design and along the detail markings. (Fig. C)

FINISH IT UP

1. Sew together the tea mat back and front, right sides together, leaving a 3" opening along a side. Clip the corners.

tip Clipping the seam allowance in the corners helps create sharper corners. Be careful not to clip the stitches!

2. Turn the tea mat right side out, using a chopstick or other similar object to help poke the corners out neatly. Press flat. Turn under the seam allowance for the opening and press well. Hand stitch the opening closed.

ADD EMBELLISHMENTS

Thread an embroidery needle with 2 strands of embroidery thread. Stitch around the edge of the coaster, about ¼" from the edge, with a running stitch (page 19). Skip over the corners. Add small X's to each of the corners. Be sure to bury any knots so they don't show on the back.

Now invite a friend over for tea to enjoy your little work of art.

Fig. A

Fig. B

Fig. C

Circle Pot Holders
Sweetwater

FINISHED POT HOLDER:
8½" diameter

We love how the colorful binding of these pot holders really "pops" next to the black and cream fabric. They make great gifts—think teachers, grandmothers, and even your mail carrier. Who couldn't use a new set of pot holders?

Photography by Farmhouse Creations, Inc.

Materials and Cutting

Makes 1 pot holder.

FABRIC FOR FRONT: 4 prints, each cut 6" × 6"

FABRIC FOR BACK: 10" × 10"

BINDING: 1 fat quarter

COTTON BATTING: 9" × 9"

INSUL-FLEECE (BY C&T PUBLISHING): 9" × 9"

SWEETWATER was founded in 2001 by Karla Eisenach and her two daughters, Lisa Burnett and Susan Kendrick. Located in Colorado, Sweetwater's simple yet sophisticated aesthetic infuses their many product lines, including fabric and quilt patterns for Moda.

WEBSITE: thesweetwaterco.com

This project originally appeared in *Sweetwater's Simple Home*, by Lisa Burnett, Karla Eisenach & Susan Kendrick, available as an eBook from Stash Books.

Instructions

See the pattern (page 54); a ¼" seam allowance is included.

1. Use the pattern to cut 4 quarter-circle pieces from the 4 prints.

2. With the right sides together, sew together 2 of the quarter-circles along a straight edge. Press. Repeat with the remaining 2 quarter-circles and press.

3. Sew together the 2 pieced half-circles to make the front. Press.

4. Layer the back, batting, Insul-Fleece, and front together.

5. Stitch close to the edge of the front through all the layers and trim away the excess back and batting.

6. Quilt the pot holder as desired. We used a flower design.

7. Bind the pot holder. (We used Continuous Bias Binding, below. Cut bias strips 2¼" wide and measuring 30" long.)

CONTINUOUS BIAS BINDING

A continuous bias involves using a square sliced in half diagonally and then sewing the triangles together so that you continuously cut marked strips to make continuous bias binding. The same instructions can be used to cut bias for piping.

Cut the fabric for the bias binding or piping so it is a square. For example, if yardage is ½ yard, cut an 18" × 18" square. Cut the square in half diagonally, creating 2 triangles.

Sew these triangles together as shown, using a ¼" seam allowance. Press the seam open.

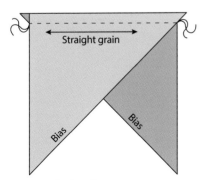

Sew triangles together.

Using a ruler, mark the parallelogram created by the 2 triangles with lines spaced the width you need to cut the bias. Cut about 5" along the first line.

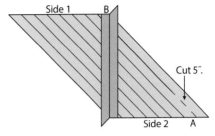

Mark lines and begin cutting.

Join side 1 and side 2 to form a tube. The raw edge at line A will align with the raw edge at B. This will allow the first line to be offset by one strip width. Pin the raw edges right sides together, making sure that the lines match. Sew with a ¼" seam allowance. Press the seam open. Cut along the drawn lines, creating one continuous strip.

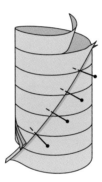

Hotty Totty Casserole Carrier

Trish Preston

FINISHED CARRIER:
Fits a 9″ × 13″ dish

Well, you Hotty Totty, you! It's kind of a naughty name for a fun casserole carrier, don't you think? Whether for the school party, a neighborhood picnic, a potluck at work, or a gathering of friends at the lake, this little carrier is both functional and great looking.

I imagine this as a great gift for a friend who is newly married or new to your neighborhood. Or maybe for a friend who is recuperating from an illness—How fabulous would it be to show up with dinner in a cute carrier that they can keep and use again?

It's easy to adjust this pattern for various sizes of pans you might have on hand and make a matching set.

Style photography by Britt Lakin; instructional photography by Diane Pedersen and Nissa Brehmer of C&T Publishing, Inc.

TRISH PRESTON is the designer and owner of Two Peas in a Pod Homegrown Designs, a company offering sewing patterns and professional inspiration. She has appeared on the PBS television show *It's Sew Easy*. Trish offers online courses through her blog. She lives near Columbus, Ohio.

WEBSITE: prestonfamilyfarms.org

This project originally appeared in *Because I Love You Sew*, by Trish Preston, available as an eBook from Stash Books.

Because **I Love You Sew**

Trish Preston

17 Handmade Gifts for Everyone in Your Life

Materials

COTTON PRINT 1 (FLORAL): 1⅜ yards for main exterior

COTTON PRINT 2 (RED STRIPE): 1⅜ yards for exterior patchwork and lining

COTTON PRINT 3 (ORANGE CHEVRON): ¼ yard for exterior patchwork

HOOK-AND-LOOP TAPE: 5½" length

METALIZED MYLAR INSULATED INTERFACING: 1 package or ¾ yard, such as Insul-Fleece (by C&T Publishing)

HARD PURSE HANDLES: A minimum of 8½" wide (I used bamboo handles 8½" × 5½".)

Cutting

COTTON PRINT 1
Cut 1 piece 7½" × 36½" for exterior panel.
Cut 1 piece 11" × 43¾" for interior panel.

COTTON PRINT 2
Cut 1 piece 3" × 36½" for exterior panel.
Cut 1 piece 11" × 43¾" for lining.
Cut 1 piece 13½" × 36½" for lining.

COTTON PRINT 3
Cut 1 piece 4½" × 36½" for exterior panel.

INSULATED INTERFACING
Cut 1 piece 11" × 43¾" for interior panel.
Cut 1 piece 13½" × 30½" for exterior panel.

Construction

Seam allowances are ⅜" unless otherwise noted.

PREPARATION

1. Sew together the 36½"-long pieces of fabrics 1, 2, and 3 to form 1 piece 13½" × 36½" for the outside of the exterior panel. Press the seams to one side.

2. Round all the corners of the exterior, interior, linings, and interior insulated interfacing pieces using the corner pattern (page 93) or a 6" saucer as a guide.

tip Sew with the insulated interfacing side up and the fabric side down on the sewing machine. The interfacing tends to stick on the sewing machine plate, and that could pull and pucker your fabric. Sewing with the fleece side up helps the feed dogs to work better.

MAKE THE INTERIOR PANEL

1. Place the interior piece right side up with the lining on top right side down. Add the insulated fleece interfacing with shiny side facing down. Pin together the layers. (**Fig. A**)

2. Sew all the way around, leaving a 7″ opening in the center of one long side for turning. Clip the curves.

3. Turn the interior panel right side out. Press and topstitch all the way around, closing the opening on the edge.

4. On the lining side, place a 1½″ piece of hook-and-loop tape on one end, centered and ½″ from the edge. Place a 4″ piece of hook-and-loop tape centered and 8″ below the bottom edge of this piece. Stitch down the hook-and-loop tape pieces. (**Fig. B**)

5. Turn this panel lining side down and, on the opposite end, place a 4″ piece of hook-and-loop tape centered and ½″ from the edge. Place a 1½″ piece of hook-and-loop tape 8″ below the lower edge of this piece. Pin the tape in place and fold over the panel to check that the pieces match up. It is helpful to place a 9″ × 13″ pan on your panel to make sure that your tape closures will work and match up. Adjust as necessary. Stitch the tape in place.

MAKE THE EXTERIOR PANEL

1. Place the exterior piece right side up with the lining on top right side down. Add the insulated fleece interfacing with shiny side facing down, centering it between the short edges. There will be 3″ of fabric extending beyond the interfacing on each end. Pin together the layers. (**Fig. C**)

2. Sew all the way around, leaving a 7″ opening in the center of one long side for turning. Clip the curves.

3. Turn the carrier right side out. Press and topstitch all the way around.

4. To hold the interfacing in place, stitch through all layers 3″ from each end. You can mark this line with an erasable marker if necessary.

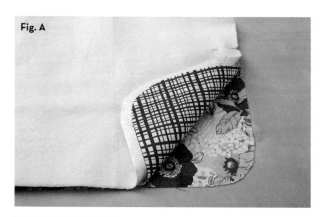

Fig. A

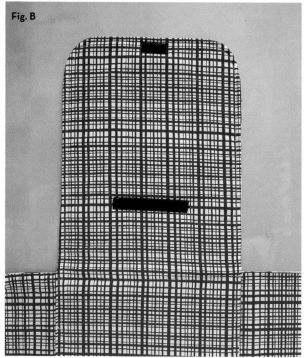

Fig. B

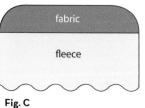

fabric

fleece

Fig. C

ADD THE HANDLE

1. Fold the 3″ of fabric that extends beyond the interfacing over the handle at the stitching line of the interfacing and toward the right side of the panel. Pin. (**Figs. D & E**)

tip Pin and then move the handle around, smoothing the fabric as you put in the next pin. It takes some wiggling to find the best angle to get the fabric pinned.

2. Sew close to the handle. Stitch slowly, continuously smoothing the fabric as you sew and moving the handle as needed. (**Fig. F**)

3. Repeat on the other side for the other handle. (**Fig. G**)

PUT IT TOGETHER

1. Fold the exterior panel in half crosswise (handle to handle) and mark the center along each side with a pin. Unfold and lay flat with lining side up.

2. Fold the interior panel lengthwise, lining side in the center. Place this fold along the center of the exterior panel you just marked with the pins. Slide the interior panel so that the end with the hook-and-loop tape on the lining side is 13″ from the edge of the exterior panel. Unfold and pin together the panels. (**Fig. H**)

3. Stitch the panels together where they cross in a box shape with double lines of stitching to secure the 2 panels in place.

tip Stitch the panels together along the top edges you can see—2 short edges from the outside and 2 long edges from the lining side. Then you can stitch a second box inside these, following your first stitching lines as a guide.

Load up your mother's secret recipe for mac-n-cheese and off to the party!

Fig. D

Fig. E

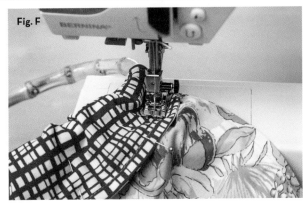

Fig. F

Fig. G

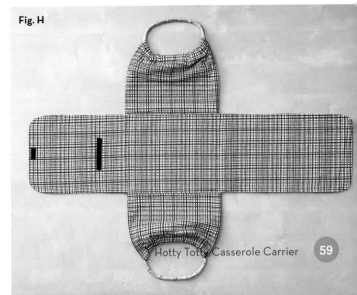

Fig. H

Grr's Chicken Scratch Apron

Kelly McCants

My Grr (grandmother) was the only person I ever knew who wore an apron. I'll never forget her making oatmeal chocolate cookies with me while wearing an aqua gingham apron. That apron and those cookies instilled a desire to create a homey life filled with memories, and Modern June is a direct result of that desire.

Just one year into Modern June we lost Grr to a long and hard fight with Alzheimer's. The night of her wake I happened upon that aqua gingham apron in my aunt Peggy's garage, tucked in an open box. Years after Grr's death, my aunt Marianne sent me a handwritten copy of the pattern that Grr used to make the beloved apron and its "chicken scratch embroidery." The instructions are jumbled and lack the details a novice stitcher would need. But there in her own handwriting, I find inspiration! I've been saving this chicken scratch apron for something special. I hope it reminds you of someone equally as wonderful as my Grr.

Photography by Meghan McSweeney

Materials and Supplies

⅝ YARD FLORAL COTTON FABRIC for apron body

⅝ YARD POLKA DOT FABRIC for waistband and ties

¼ YARD GINGHAM FABRIC for accent

1 YARD LIGHTWEIGHT SEW-IN INTERFACING, 20" wide

4 YARDS OF ½"-WIDE SINGLE-FOLD BIAS TAPE

2 SKEINS EACH OF ORANGE, WHITE, AND YELLOW EMBROIDERY FLOSS (or colors that work with your fabrics)

KELLY MCCANTS is Kelly McCants, a.k.a. Modern June, the Oilcloth Addict, learned to sew at age thirteen and has spent a lifetime stitching and drafting patterns. In college, she studied costume design and worked in film and theater costume shops all over the United States until she became a mother of two.

The McCants family lives in an 87-year-old house in a charming neighborhood in Richmond, Virginia. During their early years of parenthood, Kelly and her husband, Don, spent a lot of time restoring the house. In 2006, Kelly began homeschooling her children and started her company, Modern June, as a creative outlet. Her hand-sewn housewares business grew as quickly as the kids, with everything happening in her home until early 2013, when Modern June moved to a nearby studio space. She maintains a home studio and says it's a creative place of peace—if you don't mind the teenagers!

WEBSITE: modernjune.com

This project originally appeared in *At Home with Modern June*, by Kelly McCants, available as an eBook from Stash Books.

NOTE: JUNE SUGGESTS

My grandmother used the following design to embroider aprons for Christmas gifts for many years. She always used black and white embroidery floss on a simple gingham fabric. I'm using fresh citrus colors for my modern approach to chicken scratch. I don't think she'd mind ... too much!

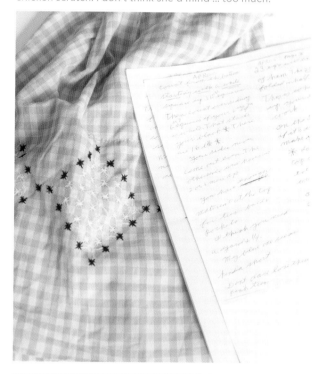

Instructions

CUTTING IT OUT

1. *From floral:* Cut 1 rectangular panel 18″ × 34¼″ for the apron body. Mark the center along 1 long side—this will be the top edge.

2. *From polka dot:* Cut 2 strips 7″ × 29″ for the apron ties and another strip 7″ × 22″ for the waistband. Cut 2 squares 7″ × 7″ for the pockets.

3. *From gingham and interfacing:* Cut 1 strip 5½″ × 34¼″ for embroidered contrast hem panel. Cut 2 rectangles 2¾″ × 7″ for the embroidered pocket trim.

EMBROIDERING IT

To learn the stitches for this project, see Hand Stitches (page 66).

Contrast Hem Panel

1. Baste the 5½″ × 34¼″ gingham piece to the matching interfacing piece. You can skip this step if the apron print won't show through the gingham. However, if the apron fabric shows through, so will the reverse stitches.

2. Fold the gingham in half horizontally to find the center-most row with white squares. Lightly press with an iron to mark this important center line; it will serve a guide throughout the handwork process.

3. With a pin, mark a white square on the center line that is approximately 1½″ away from the right-hand edge of the gingham.

4. Use a disappearing-ink marker to draw the pattern at right on the gingham, placing the rightmost snowflake in the design where the pin is.

- Draw the outer diamond of snowflakes on the white squares.

- Draw the inner snowflakes on the darker colored squares.

- Draw dashes on the lighter colored squares.

5. Place the marked section of the panel into a small embroidery hoop.

tip Be careful not to stretch the fabric.

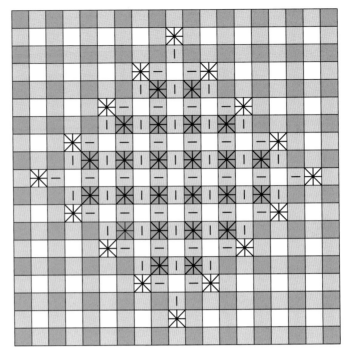

Chicken scratch diamond embroidery

6. Embroider the design with 3 strands of embroidery floss, working counterclockwise. Work in a circle, being careful to stitch the same way each time.

- Snowflake stitch (page 66) the outer diamond in orange.

- Snowflake stitch inside the diamond in white.

- Use a running stitch (page 66) in white for the dashes.

- Use the woven circle stitch (page 66) in yellow to connect groups of 4 running stitches centered on a white square.

7. Skip a solid-colored square and repeat the diamond pattern 7 times, *moving from right to left.*

Pocket Accent

1. Baste the 2¾" × 7" gingham pocket trim and matching interfacing pieces together around the outer edges.

2. Use the stitch guide (below) to create a sweet little moment on the pocket trim. Center the design on your trim piece. My top 3 snowflakes were in white squares, but yours may be different. This pocket accent piece is so small that you don't need a hoop.

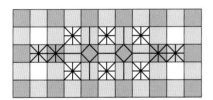

3. Stitch the snowflakes in orange, the running stitch in white, and the woven circles in yellow.

SEWING IT UP

All seam allowances are ½", unless otherwise noted.

1. Trim the top of the embroidered hem panel with bias tape. Pin and edgestitch in place.

2. Pin the panel onto the bottom edge of your apron, aligning the raw edges at the bottom. Edgestitch the top edge of the panel directly onto your apron.

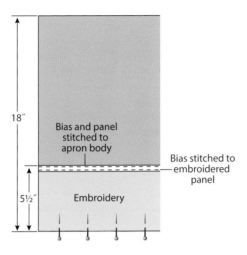

3. Sandwich the bias tape around the sides and bottom of the apron and pin into place. Edgestitch, creating *faux mitered corners* (see Bias Tape, page 66) at the bottom. Set apron aside.

4. Trim the bottom edge of both embroidered pocket accent pieces with bias tape (it's the reverse of Step 1).

5. Align the raw edges of the trimmed accent pieces with the top of each pocket, pin, and edgestitch in place along the bottom of the bias.

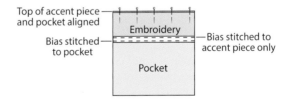

6. Pin and edgestitch bias tape to the top edges of the pockets, leaving a ½" tail on each end.

7. Place the pockets right side down on an ironing board and press ½" to the wrong side on the sides and the bottom. Tuck the extra bias trim inside the fold to create a clean pocket top. Use a clear ruler to make sure that your patch pocket is square. Reposition and re-press if not.

8. Pin each pocket to the apron 3" down from the top and 4" in from each side. Take care to tuck in the extra bias trim and the bulky folded corners; a few extra pins might be necessary. Edgestitch in place using a ⅛" seam allowance around the sides and bottoms. The top of your pocket is a high-stress area, so be sure to double-stitch the tops of the pockets on the sides. Do so by moving your needle over a click on the dial and repeating the stitching.

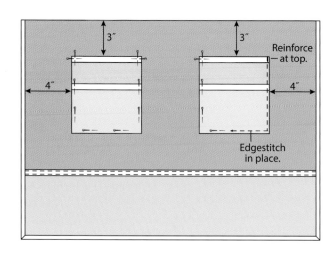

9. Machine baste along the top edge of the apron twice—first ⅜" from the raw edge and then ¼" away from the first line—to create gathering threads.

10. Pin and sew the 7" × 29" ties to each short end of the 7" × 22" waistband piece, right sides together. Press your seams open.

11. Matching the centers, pin the waistband and apron body right sides together as shown. Align the sides of the apron body with the side seams in the waistband. Pull gently on the gathering threads and slide the fabric toward the center until the apron body is the same size as the waistband. Distribute gathers evenly and pin in place. Sew the 2 together using a ½" seam allowance. Remove the gathering stitches, and press the seams up and into the waistband.

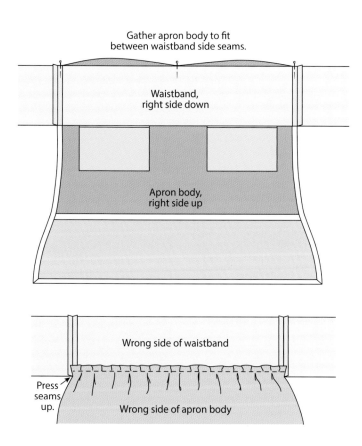

12. Fold the entire waistband in half lengthwise, right sides together. Starting at the side seams in the waistband, sew the ties closed along the bottom edges, creating a tube on each side of the apron. Draw a 45° angle at the end of each tie. Cut along this pencil line, pin, and sew shut. Turn ties right side out and press.

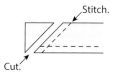

NOTE: JUNE SUGGESTS

The ties are very long so that they can wrap around the back and tie in a bow at the front of your body. If you prefer to tie a bow in the back instead, you may wish to shorten the ties appropriately.

13. With the apron wrong side down on your ironing board, fold ½" of the back side of the waistband under, enclosing the seam allowances of the apron body and the waistband. Press and pin in place. Turn the apron right side up and edgestitch the apron's waistband closed.

Now it's time to whip up a batch of no-bake oatmeal chocolate cookies with someone special!

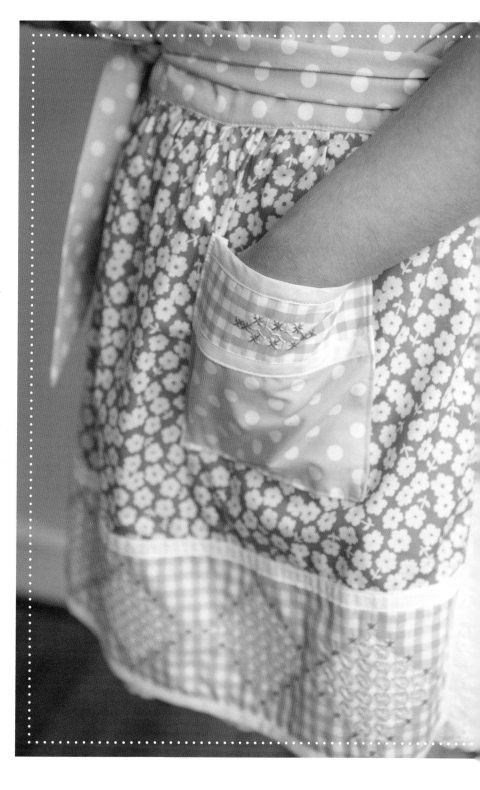

Hand Stitches

RUNNING STITCH

Start by threading your needle and knotting off the end. From the wrong side of the fabric, come up in the center of a square along the right side (A). Place the needle through to the wrong side of the fabric (B) and bring it back up to the top side (C). Repeat.

SNOWFLAKE STITCH

Also known as a double cross-stitch.

1. Thread a needle and knot the thread. Make a cross-stitch by coming up from the bottom from A to B and then from C to D. Continue to make another cross over the first by bringing the needle out through E.

2. Now go from E to F and then from G to H. Without knotting off, move on to the next snowflake stitch, moving counterclockwise in the design.

WOVEN CIRCLE STITCH

This combination is usually stitched on gingham, which provides spacing for the pattern based on the light and dark squares in the gingham weave. Each different stitch can be done in a different color, or only the woven circle itself can be made in a different color.

1. Make 2 rows of 2 snowflake stitches, each separated by a gingham square.

2. Stitch a single running stitch on each square between each pair of snowflake stitches.

3. Bring the needle to the front at the inside of a running stitch and wrap the thread around the inside ends of all 4 running stitches, twice, to create a circle. Bring the needle down through your starting point.

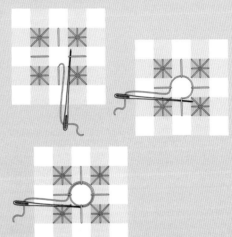

Faux Mitered Corners

When applying bias tape or oilcloth trim to a project with corners, I suggest creating a faux mitered corner. Start by sandwiching the hem within the trim or bias tape, edgestitching in place all the way to the end of the corner, and backstitching. Remove from the machine and clip threads. Open up your folded trim and tuck the bottom half under the oilcloth. This creates a 45° angle at the corner. Now close the fold, encasing the project within the trim. Make sure your corners match up and create a tidy 45° angle. Pin and edgestitch. This works for both cotton and oilcloth bias tape.

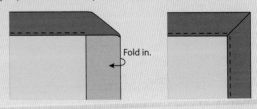

Fold in.

Appliqué Zipper Pouches

Jennifer Heynen

FINISHED POUCH:
Approx. 5″ × 6″

Decorate these zippered, appliquéd pouches with appliqués and embellishments of your choice. Make them in colors to match each of your handbags. If you have avoided zippers because they seem too hard, give this project a try! They're easier than you think!

Style photography by Nissa Brehmer and instructional photography by Diane Pedersen

JENNIFER HEYNEN It all started at age 4, when Jennifer received a child's Sew Perfect Sewing Machine. Her grandmother gave her a stack of upholstery fabric samples, and Jennifer jumped right in to sewing. In high school, her first job was at a fabric store so she could basically spend her paycheck on more fabric. Even before that, she had decided she wanted to run off to New York City and become a fashion designer. Her horizons opened when her schedule had room for another art class, where she fell in love with ceramics and went on to received a BFA in ceramics from Indiana University. She has been a self-supporting artist for 18 years, selling her ceramic tiles, beads, and jewelry.

In the back of her mind, Jennifer had always said she would go back to school to get her master's degree in textiles when she turned 36. (Why 36? It just sounded like a good number, no reason at all.) She was about to turn 36 and was considering her options for school, classes, and such, and decided she would rather design fabric more than anything. She taught herself in her free time to see where that would take her.

After a year of consistently working on her portfolio, she headed to Quilt Market with a handful of meetings with fabric companies and a stomach full of nerves and excitement. Jennifer signed a contract with In The Beginning Fabrics right after the show and continues to work with them. Currently she is designing her twelfth line of fabric for them. Alongside designing fabric, Jennifer has a line of sewing patterns and craft kits under the Jennifer Jangles name.

WEBSITE: jenniferjangles.com

This project originally appeared in *Stitch Kitsch*, by Jennifer Heynen, available as an eBook from Stash Books.

Materials

Makes 1 pouch.

¼ YARD OR A FAT QUARTER OF LINEN for outer shell

¼ YARD OR A FAT QUARTER OF COTTON QUILTING FABRIC for lining

9″ ZIPPER OR LONGER (Zipper is trimmed later to fit.)

⅛ YARD OF 17″-WIDE PAPER-BACKED FUSIBLE WEB

ASSORTED FABRICS FOR APPLIQUÉ (approx. 4–8 fabrics measuring 4″ × 4″)

8″ OF POM-POM TRIM, 5 FELT BALLS 1.5cm (¾″), or 24″ OF SARI RIBBON for embellishing

3″ OF RIBBON ¼″–½″ wide for split ring loop

1″ SPLIT RING

3 SMALL BUTTONS ¼″–⅓″ in diameter for flower pouch

ALL-PURPOSE SEWING THREAD to match outer shell fabric

BLACK ALL-PURPOSE SEWING THREAD for decorative topstitching

NONSTICK PRESSING CLOTH

Optional: ¼ YARD OF FLANNEL to add padding and weight to the bag

Cutting

OUTER SHELL
2 pieces 5½″ × 6½″

LINING
2 pieces 5½″ × 6½″

IF USING SARI RIBBON TRIM
5–8 pieces 3″ long

FLANNEL (OPTIONAL)
2 pieces 5½″ × 6½″

Instructions

Seam allowances are ¼".

1. Trace Appliqué Pattern 1, 2, 3, or 4 (pages 94 and 95) onto the paper side of the fusible web.

....

NOTE: All appliqué images have been reversed and are ready for tracing.

....

2. Cut out the fusible web approximately ¼" outside the drawn line. Place the appliqué fabric right side down on the ironing board. Place the fusible web on top of the fabric, paper side up. Be sure the fabric is larger than the fusible web. To protect your iron, cover the fusible with a nonstick pressing cloth. Follow the manufacturer's instructions to adhere the web to your fabric. Repeat for each piece of the appliqué pattern. Trim on the pattern lines and remove paper backing.

Arrange all pieces on an outer shell piece, keeping them at least ¼" inside the edge. Iron in place.

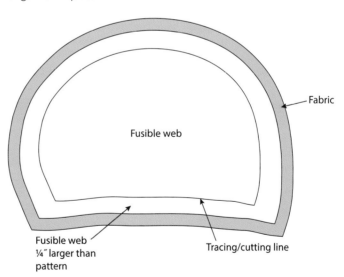

3. Topstitch around the appliqués approximately ⅛" from the edges using black thread.

4. If you're making the flower pouch, hand sew the buttons as indicated on the pattern.

5. When the appliqué is finished, it's time to add the zipper. Start with one of the outer shell pieces right side up on your cutting surface. Place the zipper, teeth down, across the top of the fabric with the far edge of the zipper along the edge of the fabric, and so that both ends extend past the edges. Pin in place. (Your zipper might seem too long, but be patient. This technique makes adding a zipper a breeze!)

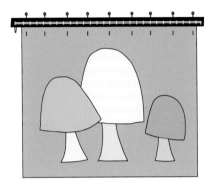

6. Place a piece of the lining fabric, right side down, on top of the pinned zipper. Make sure to match the top and side edges of the outer shell and lining. Pin the lining fabric in place.

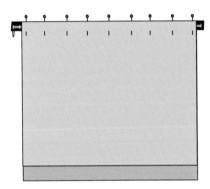

7. Sew using the zipper foot on your sewing machine.

 tip

• Dropping the feed dogs on the sewing machine and using a free-motion foot can be helpful but is not necessary.

• If your stitching misses an edge or gets a little wobbly, stitch back over that part. There is nothing wrong with going over the stitches a few times; it adds detail.

8. Fold the fabric back from the zipper so that the outer shell and lining are wrong sides together. Place the remaining side of the zipper face down onto the right side of the remaining outer shell piece. Align outer shell fabric sides with the fabrics sewn in Step 7. Pin in place.

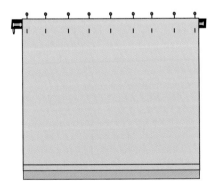

9. Place the lining, right side down, on top of the zipper. Make sure to match the top and side edges of the outer shell and lining fabrics. Pin in place and sew.

10. Thread the ribbon through the spilt ring and fold the ribbon in half so that the ends meet and the right side is facing out. Pin together. On the front side of the outer shell, measure approximately 1″ down from the zipper on the side with the zipper pull. Pin the loop so the ring is toward the center of the bag.

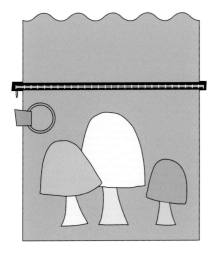

tip Make sure the metal ring is in at least ½″ from the raw edge of the bag, or else it will be in the way when you sew. The ribbon edges are intended to be longer on the inside of the bag; therefore, don't try to align the edges with the raw edges of the bag. The ribbon is longer to ensure that it doesn't come unraveled and come loose from your bag.

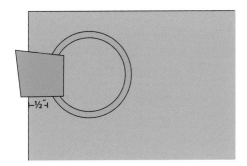

11. If you are using sari ribbon or pom-pom trim, pin it across the bottom of the front of the bag, with the trims facing inward.

12. Unzip the zipper approximately two-thirds of the way. Place the 2 outer fabrics right sides together and the 2 lining pieces right sides together. When you are ready to pin the zipper sides, fold the zipper in half so that the teeth are on the fold. Make sure the teeth of the zipper are facing the outer bag fabric pieces.

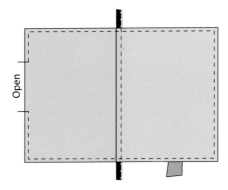

13. Sew around all of the edges, leaving a 3″ section open at the bottom of the lining for turning. Clip the corners, taking care not to clip the stitching. Cut off all of the excess zipper and trim.

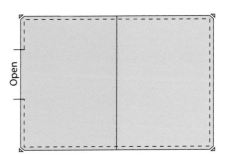

14. Turn the pouch right side out. Hand stitch the opening closed. Push the lining inside the bag and press.

15. If you're making the camper bag, hand stitch the felt balls onto the bottom.

tip For an extra touch, you can attach ribbons, pom-poms, or beads to the zipper pull.

1-2 Sucker Pouch

Angie Wilson

FINISHED POUCH:
9″ wide × 3″ high × 3″ deep

Zipper pouches are easy to whip up in an afternoon (even as a last-minute gift before a party). They're small enough to use for practicing different techniques and also great for showing off favorite fabrics.

I love this style of zipper pouch. It provides four sides to showcase fabric, and it has enough room to stow an overabundant pen collection (not that any of us has one of those).

Style photography by Lucy Glover and instructional photography by Diane Pedersen of C&T Publishing, Inc.

ANGIE WILSON lives in the capital of Australia, Canberra, with her very understanding husband and her curious son. Angie is a passionate creative who loves fabric the way that Carrie Bradshaw loves shoes. She's got a weakness for trashy television, processed sugar, and hugs from her boys.

Angie has been blogging since 2002 and can't imagine life without some form of writing in it. Her blog name, "GnomeAngel," arose from a weird obsession with collecting gnomes, her first tattoo, and a friend who thought she was (g)no(me) angel. Angie strongly believes that everyone should make time and space for being creative.

WEBSITE: gnomeangel.com

This project originally appeared in *Fussy Cutters Club*, by Angie Wilson, available from Stash Books.

Materials

Depending on the prints you choose, the frequency of the repeats, and how you choose to fussy cut, you may need more fabric than indicated in the materials list.

FUSSY-CUT FABRICS: A mix to total ½ yard

LINING: 1 fat quarter

BACKING: 1 fat quarter of flannel

BATTING: ½ yard

10″ ZIPPER

DECORATIVE ZIPPER PULL (*optional*)

CLOVER WONDER CLIPS (*optional*)

NOTE: I used leftover quilt batting and flannel to make this pouch because these materials hold their shape, but you can also use fusible fleece interfacing and a quilting cotton backing for the quilted panel. The upside of that combination is that it isn't as thick as batting and flannel, so it won't be as puffy and cumbersome to turn right side out. However, over time, fusible fleece loses its rigidity and shape a lot quicker than batting and flannel.

Cutting

LINING

Cut 1 square 12½″ × 12½″.

Cut 1 square 2″ × 2″ for the zipper tabs.

BACKING

Cut 1 square 13½″ × 13½″.

BATTING

Cut 1 square 13½″ × 13½″.

Construction

Seam allowances are ¼″ unless otherwise noted. Press seams open or to the side. Refer to Tutorial: How to Improvisationally Fussy Cut (page 79) for detailed instructions on improvisational fussy cutting.

1. Using improvisational fussy cutting and piecing techniques, construct a slab of fabric measuring 13½″ × 13½″. Refer to the panel cutting diagram (right) to rotate your prints so that they will be oriented in the correct direction when the pouch is finished, taking full advantage of your fussy-cut fabrics.

tip **Caution!**

Pay attention to the direction of your prints while piecing. Because of the way the fabric wraps around the pouch, prints may appear upside down if you aren't careful! Refer to the panel cutting diagram (right) so you do not place any fussy-cut prints in areas that will be trimmed away.

2. Sandwich the fabric panel, interfacing, batting, and flannel. Quilt the panel as desired. Trim to 12½″ × 12½″.

3. Make a pattern, or mark the quilted panel following the panel cutting diagram below. Trim away the corners of the panel and the 12½″ lining piece using the pattern. Set aside.

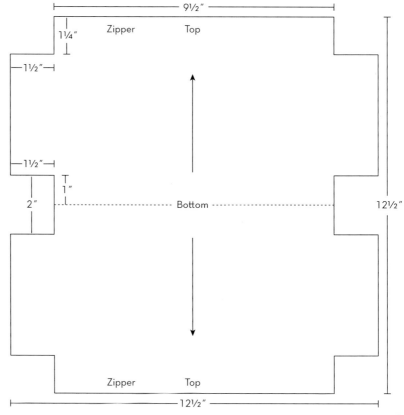

Panel cutting

4. Fold the 2″ × 2″ lining square in half, wrong sides together. Topstitch ⅛″ from the fold. The piece will now measure 2″ × 1″. Cut it in half to make 2 squares 1″ × 1″ for the zipper tabs.

Cut.

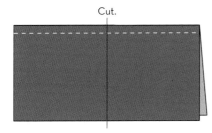

5. To place the zipper tabs correctly, align the zipper, centered and with the teeth facing up, with the top 9½″ edge of the quilted panel. Place the zipper tabs on top of just the zipper, with the topstitching toward the center of the zipper, aligning the raw edges of the tabs with the inner corners of the panel as shown. Make sure the zipper head is between the tabs. Baste the tabs in place along both outer edges of the zipper tape. Trim the excess zipper.

Baste tabs.

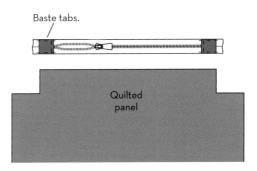

Quilted panel

 **Fear Not Zippers**

Zippers are really easy to insert—especially if you read your sewing machine manual and use the right sewing machine foot. Once you nail your first one, there will be no stopping you.

Fussy Designing

When I work with improvisational fussy cutting, I like to choose a focal print and then build a color story based on that print. Working this way makes fabric selection a lot easier and creates a cohesive look.

The side of the pouch that's on display measures roughly 3″ × 9″. Using a print that is approximately 3″ high in this area will make it a feature on the side of your pouch. Alternatively, you can use a feature print that is a lot larger and wrap it around the pouch to great effect.

I like to work with a mix of prints that range in scale from 1″ to 5″ in finished height when making this project. If you wrap a large print around the pouch, choose a relatively narrow one so it doesn't overpower the piecing on the pouch.

You could use the focal print as the start of your story and pick other print motifs that work with this narrative. I like to use the colors in my focal print to build a color palette. Regardless of how you develop your design, work toward a balance of focal prints, blenders, and solids.

6. Place the zipper on top of the 9½" top edge of the panel again, right sides together, with the zipper pull facedown and to the left. Pin and baste the zipper in place. (You can skip the basting if you are confident working with zippers.)

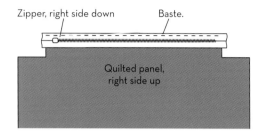

tip **Better Than Pinning**

I don't like to use pins when inserting zippers because I can never get them to stay where I want them. Instead, I use Clover Wonder Clips to keep the panel, zipper, and lining in place while I work. I find these are much more reliable and a lot easier to maneuver. Remember, Clover Wonder Clips will not pass under the foot of your sewing machine, so you will need to remove them as you stitch.

7. Place the lining, with the right side facing down, on top of the zipper and panel.

Pin and stitch in place.

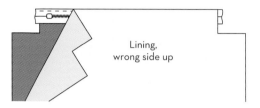

8. Flip the lining out of the way, and fold the quilted panel, right sides together, up to the opposite side of the zipper tape to form a loop. Pin and baste the zipper in place on the panel (ignore the lining for now).

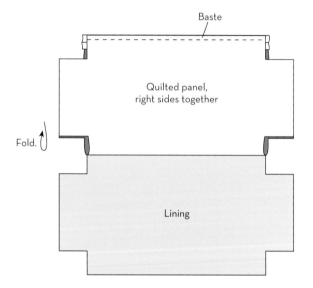

9. Fold the lining right sides together, and align the unattached 9½" edge of the lining with the edge of the zipper that does not have lining attached. This will create a loop out of the lining. Pin and stitch the lining to the zipper and the panel. You will have a panel loop and a lining loop, both attached at the zipper.

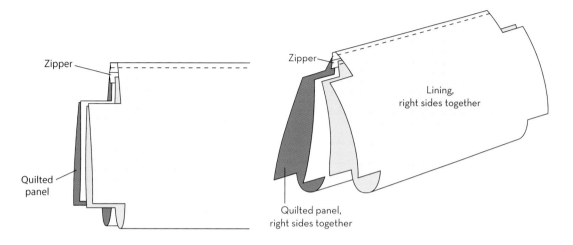

10. Open the zipper halfway. Pull apart the lining and panel so that the lining is facing itself, right sides together, and the panel is also facing itself, right sides together. Stitch down the sides of the pouch in 4 places, as shown. Press open the seams.

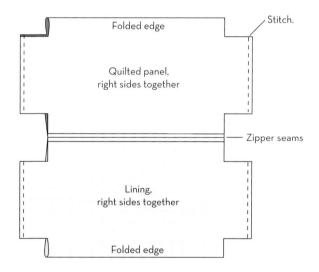

11. Pinch together the top corners of the pouch, centering the seams on the zipper, so the corners flatten out into a straight line. Stitch together the lining and the panel at the corners; make sure to catch the zipper in the seam.

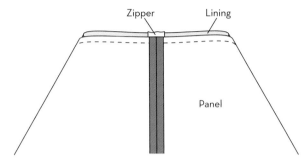

12. Pinch together the bottom corners of just the panel and stitch together. Do not stitch together the lining corners.

13. Gently turn the pouch right side out through the unsewn lining corners. Pull the lining out and pinch the lining corners together into a flat line, folding the raw edges ¼" inside. Topstitch the lining corners closed and push the lining back inside the pouch.

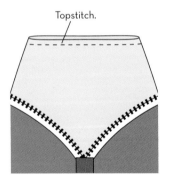

tip **Avoid a Trapezoid**

Measure the length of the first top corner seam. Make sure all the remaining exterior corner seams are the same length, so the ends are square. You may need to mark a new seamline further in from the raw edges of the corner.

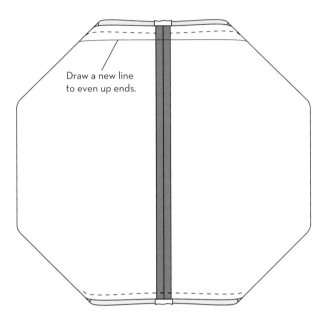

Draw a new line to even up ends.

Tutorial: How to Improvisationally Fussy Cut

This technique is based on the concept of creating a slab, where you sew together bits of fabric to make a larger piece of fabric. I use this technique a lot when making pillows and bags, but you can replace any piece of fabric in a design with a slab.

I like to stick to a color palette and use tones from that range to create a cohesive look. I've seen this technique used successfully, however, with a rainbow of colors and prints.

MATERIALS

Fabrics • Ruler • Rotary cutter • Cutting mat

1. Start with a feature print that you'd like to highlight. Cut out the motif, noting the measurements. In this example, the motif is cut as a rectangle. Make sure you leave enough of a border so that you don't lose any of the desired motif to the seam allowance. (Fig. A)

2. Cut and sew a piece of fabric to any side of the rectangle. Press and trim the piece if needed to fit the fussy-cut motif. (Fig. B)

3. Select another fussy-cut piece, and add it to the slab. If it's smaller than the slab, add improv pieces to enlarge it. Press and trim. (Fig. C)

4. Continue in this manner, alternating sides and staggering the seams. Press and trim as you go, until the slab is the desired size. (Fig. D)

5. Staystitch ⅛" in from the edge to secure the seams. (Fig. E)

Fig. A

Fig. B

Fig. C

Fig. D

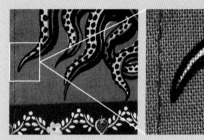
Fig. E

Clear Window Zippy Pouch

Jennifer Pol Colin

Clear vinyl offers so many possibilities for sewing projects! And when it's combined with nice fabrics and cute prints, it's even better. Stuff the front window with souvenirs, glitter, or sequins, and your zippy pouch will be the fanciest one of all!

Photography by Jennifer Pol Colin

JENNIFER POL COLIN A native of France and former expatriate in the United States, Jennifer ran Little Print Fabrics Studio in San Diego, California, where kids and grown-ups love to sew creatively.

When Jennifer arrived in the USA with 3 very little girls and an old 220V sewing machine, she was amazed by the sewing and craft supplies readily available in her new adoptive country and didn't wait to sew for her new home and her family. She sewed as she never sewed before, and she started sharing her sewing journey through a blog named "My Little Print Fabrics." She quickly had the opportunity to teach craft and sewing classes in schools and was happy to discover there was a new generation of very creative girls eager to learn how to sew.

Teaching sewing appeared to be a new vocation for Jennifer. Consistently inspired by her 3 daughters, she designed unique patterns for young sewers. Her hobby quickly turned into a full-time career.

Her book, *Sew Creative*, takes up the challenge to successfully mix creativity, playful ideas, and technical sewing skills.

BLOG: mylittleprintfabrics.com

This project originally appeared in *Sew Creative*, by Jennifer Pol Colin, available from FunStitch Studio.

What You Need

HEAVYWEIGHT COTTON, 1 rectangle 11″ × 8½″ for back

and

MEDIUM-WEIGHT COTTON PRINT, 1 rectangle 11″ × 8½″ for lining (*Note: The lining will be visible through the clear vinyl.*)

Another option: Use 2 rectangles 11″ × 8½″ of heavyweight cotton for back and lining.

CLEAR VINYL, 1 rectangle 11″ × 8½″ for front

ZIPPER, 11″ length

MATCHING CORD, 7″ length (to attach to zipper pull)

ZIPPER PRESSER FOOT

SMALL BINDER CLIPS

1 SHEET 8½″ × 11″ PAPER as a pattern

TINY SPECIAL ITEMS TO FILL THE CLEAR WINDOW POUCH, such as glitter, little toys, tiny gems, seashells … (*Note: Don't select anything organic that could mold or anything sharp that could rip the plastic!*)

Prepare the Pieces

1. Use the sheet of paper as a pattern. The 8½″ edges will be the sides, and the 11″ edges will be top and bottom of the pouch. Place the pattern on the heavyweight cotton, short edge along the grainline. Trace and cut.

2. For the lining, repeat with the same fabric or a medium-weight cotton print, which will be visible through the clear vinyl.

3. To trace and cut the vinyl, lay the heavyweight cotton piece on the table and place the vinyl on top. Tape the vinyl to the table. With a ruler and a marker, trace the rectangle onto the vinyl. Cut with craft scissors.

Step by Step

It's easy to make ³/₈″–¹/₂″ seam allowances: Just line up the edge of a regular sewing foot with the edge of the fabric.

1. Place the vinyl on the right side of the lining. With the right side of the zipper (zipper teeth popping up) facing the vinyl, align the zipper tape to the top edge of the vinyl. Attach these 3 layers with binder clips. Don't use pins; it's too thick and you don't want to puncture the vinyl. (**Fig. A**)

2. Attach a zipper presser foot to the sewing machine. Position it to fall to the right of the zipper on the zipper tape. Move the needle as far to the left as possible so that it will pass freely through the left hole of the presser foot but not so far left that the needle will break on the zipper coils. Also, stitching too close to the zipper teeth can prevent the slider from moving smoothly over the zipper.

3. Sew a straight line next to the zipper teeth, pulling the binder clips off as you sew. Backstitch at the beginning and end of the stitching. (**Fig. B**)

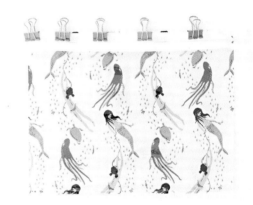

Fig. A

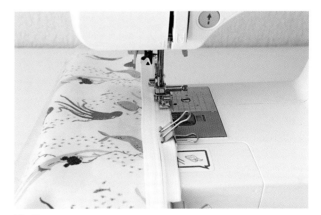

Fig. B

tip You will need to move the zipper slider out of the way as you sew. Start the stitching with a closed zipper. As you approach the slider, secure the needle position by dropping the machine's needle down. Then lift the presser foot to move the zipper slider past the needle to the side you've already sewn. Finish the stitching.

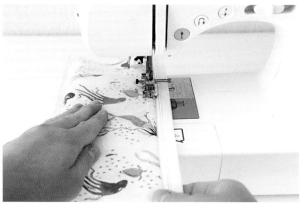
Fig. C

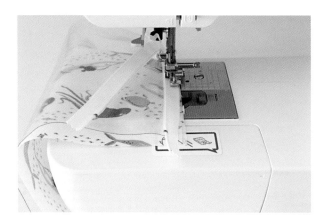

4. Open the seam and fold the layers away from the zipper. You can feel the rigidity of the vinyl. To keep it flat and pretty, finger-press the vinyl at the seamline. Use a nonstick presser foot and a large straight stitch to topstitch through all layers along the zipper. *(Note: If you don't have a nonstick pressure foot, you can just use a piece of washi tape on a regular presser foot.)* (**Fig. C**)

5. Align the heavyweight cotton back, right sides together to the other side of the zipper. No need for paper clips this time—you can pin fabric and zipper together or use double-sided fusible tape. (**Fig. D**)

6. Repeat Step 3 to attach the zipper to the back. Topstitching the back to the zipper is optional.

7. Turn the pouch to the right side and move the zipper slider to the halfway point. Fold the pouch in half at the zipper, matching the front and back rectangles, right sides together. Pin from the zipper down each side and along the bottom of the pouch where you will leave a 3″ no-sew zone. You will need this gap to fill the vinyl window with the embellishments. (**Fig. E**)

Fig. D

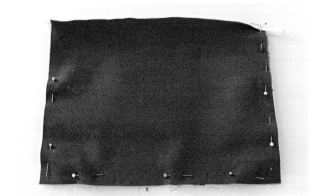
Fig. E

8. Sew across the folded zipper and down the sides; pivot at the corner and stitch up to the no-sew zone. Backstitch at the beginning and end of the stitching, and repeat on the other side of the pouch.

9. Pour some glitter or any other embellishment you would like into the pouch between the clear vinyl and the lining. Make sure you are using the right layers—not the back and the lining by mistake—otherwise you would be pouring embellishments on the floor! Do not overfill the space. (Fig. F)

10. Once the pouch is filled, go back to the machine and stitch the no-sew zone closed, completing the bottom seam. Finish the 3 sides of the pouch by zigzagging along the raw edges. This will prevent fraying.

11. Turn the pouch right side out through the zipper and push the corners out. It's not as easy as it was with past projects because of the rigidity of the vinyl.

Optional: Attach a cute piece of string or tassel to the zipper pull.

You are done!

Check it out and see how pretty the embellishments look through the window!

Fig. F

Gallery

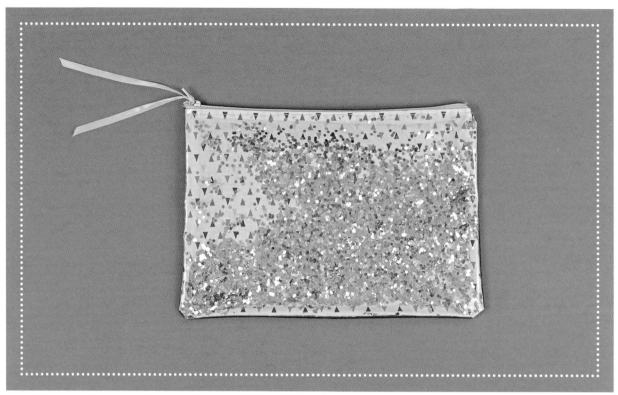

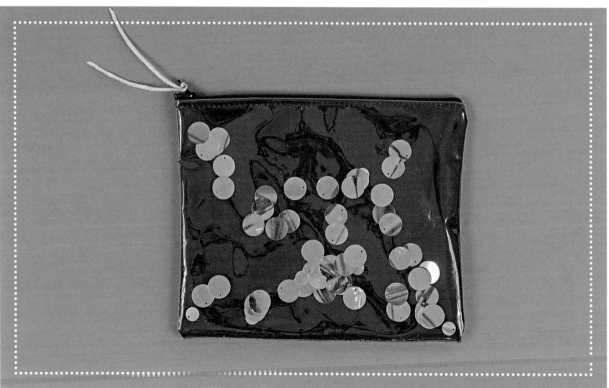

Notepad Cover

Sweetwater

Remember those old book covers you were required to slip on your junior high science books? Try this updated version—a little more stylish and a lot more fun. Two inside pockets hold two standard 5˝ × 8˝ notepads; a magnetic closure keeps them secure.

Photography by Farmhouse Creations, Inc.

Materials and Cutting

Makes 1 cover to hold 2 notepads.

FABRIC FOR OUTSIDE, LINING, AND CLOSURE TAB: ⅓ yard

FABRIC FOR POCKETS: ⅓ yard

COTTON BATTING: 14" × 11"

IRON-ON FABRIC LABEL: Or 1 sheet iron-on inkjet-printable fabric

½" MAGNETIC SNAP

NOTEPADS: 2, sized 5" × 8"

tip Helpful Hint

You can buy iron-on labels from Sweetwater that can be custom printed with any words you choose. As an alternative to these, you can use inkjet-printable fabric with iron-on adhesive on the back.

SWEETWATER was founded in 2001 by Karla Eisenach and her two daughters, Lisa Burnett and Susan Kendrick. Located in Colorado, Sweetwater's simple yet sophisticated aesthetic infuses their many product lines, including fabric and quilt patterns for Moda.

WEBSITE: thesweetwaterco.com

This project originally appeared in *Sweetwater's Simple Home,* by Lisa Burnett, Karla Eisenach & Susan Kendrick, available as an eBook from Stash Books.

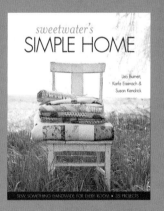

Instructions

See the pattern (page 95); a ¼″ seam allowance is included.

OUTSIDE AND BATTING

1. Cut 1 piece 12½″ × 9½″ from the outside fabric.

2. With the right side up, center the outside piece over the cotton batting.

3. Baste the outside fabric and the cotton batting together, close to the raw edge.

4. Trim away the excess batting and treat the two pieces as one.

LABEL

1. To make the fabric labels using a computer and iron-on inkjet-printable fabric, follow the instructions of the printable-fabric manufacturer to make a label measuring 1″ × 3″.

2. Peel off the paper backing (if there is one) from the label and iron it to the center of the outside piece with the label positioned vertically.

3. Stitch close around the edge of the label.

LINING AND POCKETS

1. Cut 1 piece 12½″ × 9½″ from the lining fabric.

2. Cut 1 pocket piece 12½″ × 12″ from the pocket fabric.

3. Fold the pocket piece in half with the wrong sides together, matching the 12½″ sides. Press.

4. Place the folded pocket piece over the lining piece, matching the raw edges at the sides and bottom.

5. Baste the pocket to the lining close to the raw edges.

6. Stitch down the center of the pocket to form 2 pockets, as shown.

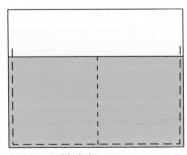

Baste pocket to lining.

CLOSURE TAB

1. Use the pattern to cut 2 pieces for the tab. Cut a piece of batting 3½″ × 5″.

2. With right side up, center 1 tab piece over the cotton batting.

3. Baste the fabric and batting together, close to the raw edge. Trim away the excess batting. This will be the underside of the tab.

4. Apply 1 part of the magnetic closure to the underside of the tab according to the manufacturer's directions. Position the magnet closure in the center and ¾″ in from the edge.

5. With the right sides together, place the remaining tab piece over the underside piece. Sew the pieces together, leaving the straight side open.

6. Trim the seam allowance to ⅛″.

7. Turn the closure tab right side out and press.

8. Topstitch close to the edge.

9. Center the tab along the left 9½″ edge of the outside piece, with the underside facing up. Baste in place.

10. Apply the second part of the magnet closure to the opposite side on the outside cover, placing the closure in the center and 1″ in from the edge.

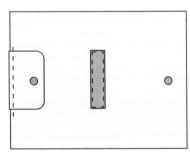

Baste tab to cover.

FINISHING

1. With the right sides together, pin the lining to the outside.

2. Trim all the corners to make them rounded.

3. Sew the lining and the outside cover together all around the edge, leaving a 3" opening at the bottom.

4. Turn the piece right side out through the opening and press.

5. Topstitch close to the edge around the entire cover. This will secure the opening closed.

6. Insert a notepad into each pocket.

Patterns

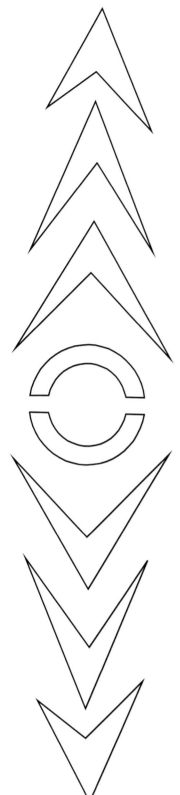

Equinox Greeting Cards

(page 4)

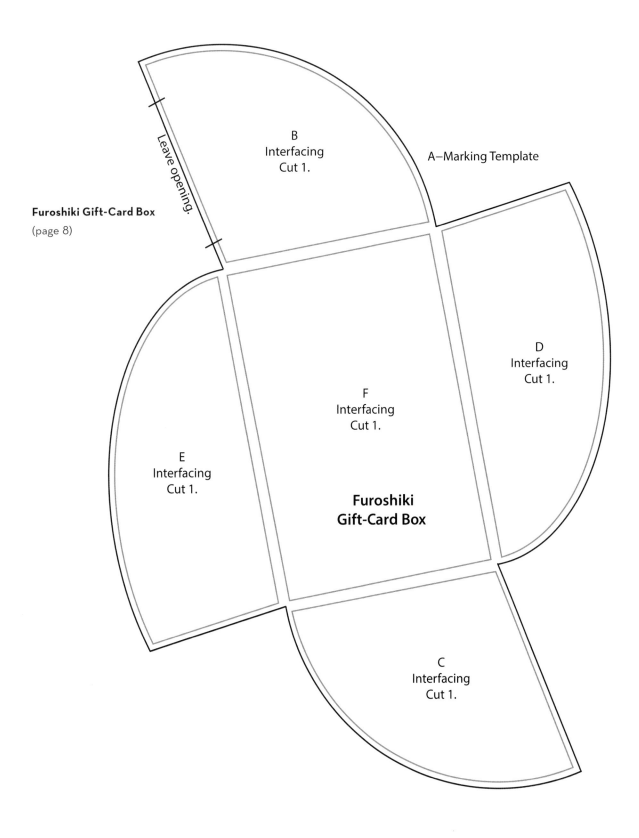

Furoshiki Gift-Card Box
(page 8)

Leave opening.

B
Interfacing
Cut 1.

A—Marking Template

D
Interfacing
Cut 1.

F
Interfacing
Cut 1.

E
Interfacing
Cut 1.

**Furoshiki
Gift-Card Box**

C
Interfacing
Cut 1.

True North Tote

(page 13)

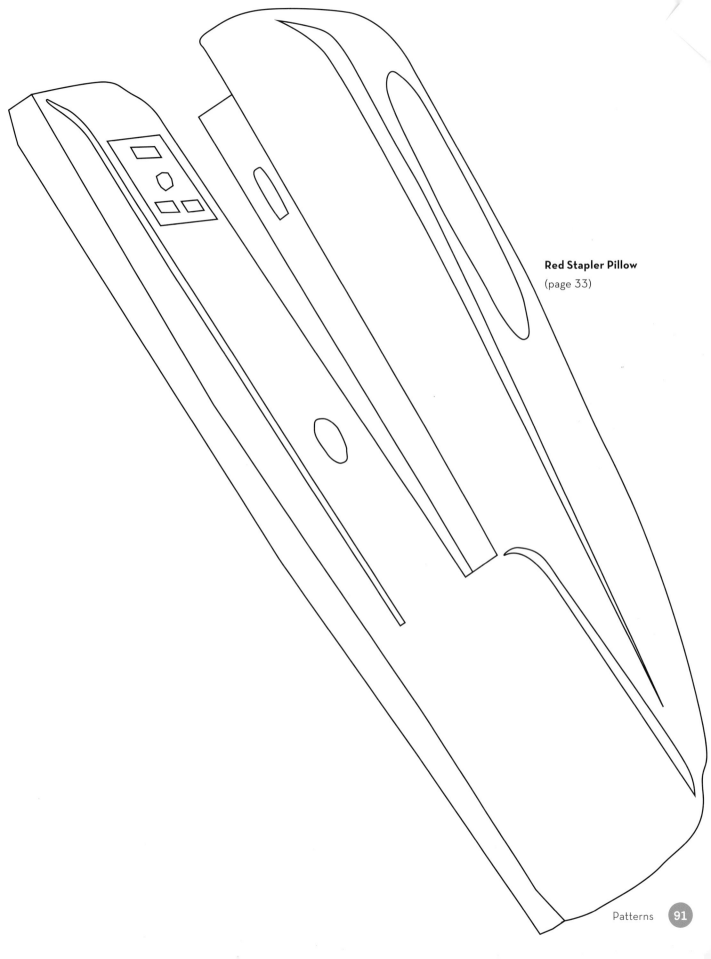

Red Stapler Pillow
(page 33)

Linen Table Runner

(page 49)

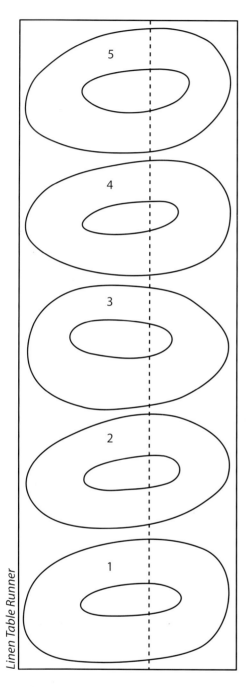

Linen Table Runner

Enlarge 200% or download full size from
tinyurl.com/11498-patterns-download.

Tea Mat

(page 52)

These patterns are reversed for iron-on transfer.

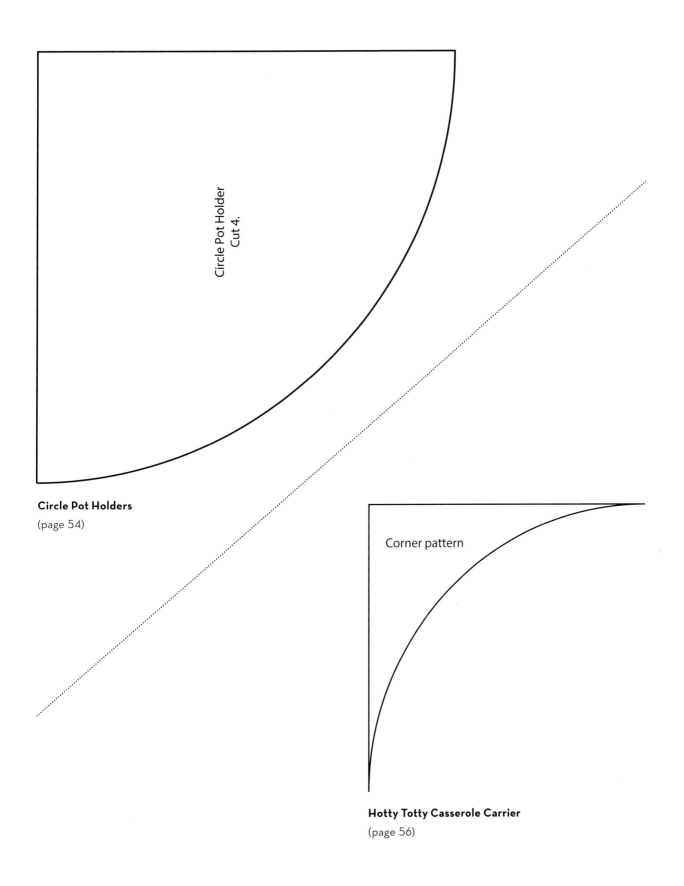

Circle Pot Holder
Cut 4.

Circle Pot Holders
(page 54)

Corner pattern

Hotty Totty Casserole Carrier
(page 56)

Appliqué Zipper Pouches

(page 67)

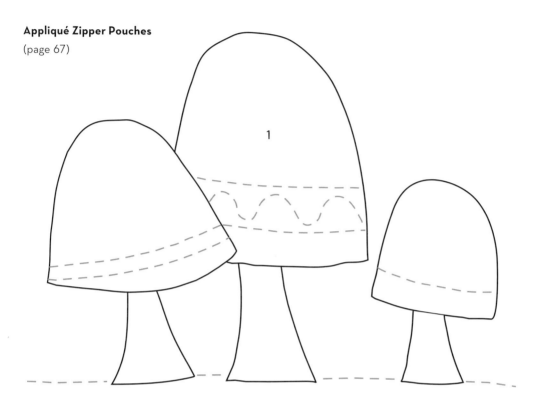

All appliqué images have been reversed and are ready for tracing.

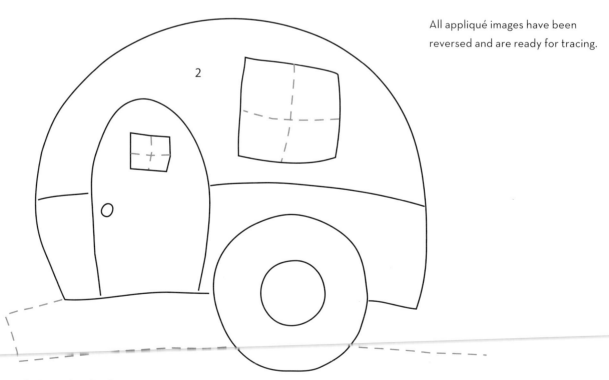

Appliqué Zipper Pouches

(page 67)

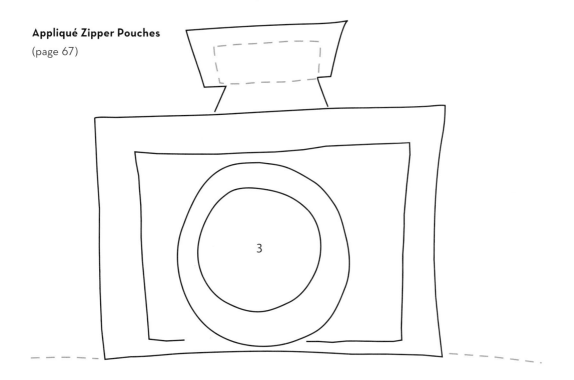

All appliqué images have been reversed and are ready for tracing.

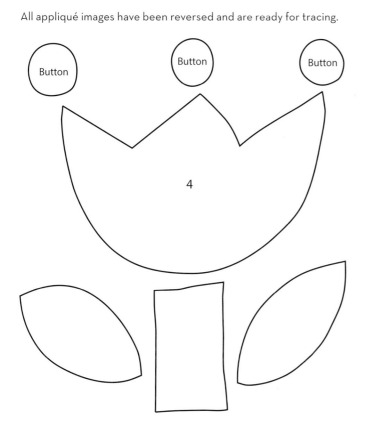

Button

Button

Button

4

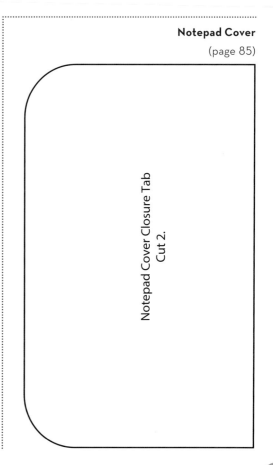

Notepad Cover

(page 85)

Notepad Cover Closure Tab
Cut 2.